Data Analysis with SPSS®

Stephen A. Sweet
State University of New York at Potsdam

Allyn & Bacon
Boston • London • Toronto • Sydney • Tokyo • Singapore

Contents

Preface

According to former Labor Secretary Robert Reich, the most successful workers in the 21st century will be those who are able to understand various forms of information and produce meaning from it (Reich 1991). Reich calls these people symbolic analysts, and they occupy positions as academics, researchers, corporate investors, managers, and programmers. What all of these jobs share in common is the need for professionals who have the ability to understand complex information and develop meaning from it. Simply open up the most current issue of *U.S. News and World Report*, *USA Today*, or *Newsweek* and you are likely to find a page devoted simply to statistics of one form or another. Statistics are important to our jobs and our culture.

Engaging in statistical analysis, contrary to popular belief, can be fun. This may be a surprise to many who have "suffered" through an introduction to statistics course. Traditionally, students learn about statistics by calculating numbers which indicate things such as Z scores, means, and chi square statistics. While there is a place for traditional statistics courses, I believe that many lose sight of the purpose of statistics as a consequence. For social scientists, our reason for studying statistics is only a means to an end. Our interest is in using data to understand social behavior, not calculating statistics for statistic's sake. Thankfully there are currently a number of computer programs on the market which take the pain out of engaging in data analysis. This book is devoted to exploring some of the capacities of one of the most popular of these programs, the **Statistical Package for the Social Sciences (SPSS)**.

This book is intended to develop capacities to critically analyze data using a tool used by professional researchers. The chapters and exercises in this book demonstrate the approach professional researchers use to make sense out of quantitative (numerical) data. This book is not intended as a "how to" manual for SPSS, but rather as a guidebook toward developing the skills necessary for quantitative data analysis and report writing. I have included many examples and exercises which show how to use the SPSS program, how to explore relationships between variables, · and how to write an independent research report.

Exercises are not intended simply to be technical tasks. Included with this book is a disk containing two data sets, rich with information concerning social behavior. One of these data sets contains over 400 different variables representing state level data. These data enable analysis of causes and consequences of variation in education, criminality, welfare use, health care, taxation, births, mortality, and environmental well-being. The other data set contains nearly 100 variables from the 1996 General Social Survey conducted by the Roper Center for Public Opinion. These data enable analysis of variation in individual experiences and attitudes relating to subjects such as education, religion, politics, sexuality, race, and taxation. Ultimately, the skills learned in this book can be applied to independent analysis of these data sets to produce research reports.

This book is divided into nine chapters, each with specific goals. Chapter 1 examines the key concepts and approaches social scientists use to conduct empirical research. Chapter 2 is an orientation to SPSS, how it operates, and how data can be loaded into the program. Chapter 3 discusses the various ways in which single variables can be examined with SPSS. Chapter 4 then discusses the ways in which relationships between two variables can be analyzed and also introduces measures of statistical significance. Chapter 5 revisits issues raised in previous chapters, explaining how relationships can be graphically depicted using SPSS. Chapter 6 and Chapter 7 explain the advantages and methods of engaging in multivariate analysis through ordinary least squares regression and logistical regression. Chapter 8 steps away from SPSS in order to discuss the structure and content of well-written research reports. Chapter 9 concludes with some ideas for research projects which can be pursued using the data provided with this book. Appendixes are included which describe the content of the data sets included with this book.

Do I Have What it Takes and What Will I Accomplish?

There is something about statistics which seems to spark fear. Computers do likewise. Put the two together and dread may result. This is unfortunate and I believe unnecessary. I expect some readers (possibly you?) may have a few concerns at this point. Some may be wondering if they need to know how to use a computer to get through the exercises in this book. The short answer is yes, but there is no time like the present to learn! Prior computer experience would be of help, but a basic understanding of how to navigate in a Windows environment will be sufficient to work through the exercises in this book.

Some readers may be concerned that they lack the requisite skills in statistics or math. This text is designed to help you become refined in analyzing quantitative data, so existing skills in statistics and math can certainly be a help. However, the text is designed to teach basic statistical inference. Therefore, no prior statistics course is needed to be able to work through the exercises in this book and only modest mathematical capabilities are needed to perform the exercises in this text.

Possibly others may be wondering why they should bother with this book if they don't plan to become statisticians or social science researchers. On one level, there may be direct benefits. All of us live in a world in which numbers are used to explain our experiences. Even if one becomes an artist or musician, the ability to read statistics critically facilitates making important decisions such as where to locate one's family, what political candidates to vote for, and what drugs should be avoided. In all likelihood SPSS will not be used to make these decisions, but you will be developing skills in quantitative data analysis which can contribute to informed decisions in this regard. At a deeper level, though, this book will help you to develop a critical perspective on how to evaluate arguments based upon quantitative data. Indeed, the real aim of this book is not teaching SPSS, but to cultivate the skills needed to be a critical consumer of information and to whet the appetite for empirical inquiry.

References and Further Reading

Reich, Robert. 1991. *The Work of Nations: Preparing Ourselves for 21ˢᵗ Century Capitalism.* New York: Alfred Knopf.

Acknowledgments

No project such as this is an individual effort. Unfortunately social convention dictates that only one or a few individuals can put their name on the cover of a book. In the customary fashion, I will offer short mention of friends and colleagues who have made immeasurable contributions. Scott Morgan and Kathleen O'Leary Morgan were exceedingly generous in allowing me to reproduce the data presented in their outstanding books *State Rankings 1997* and *Crime State Rankings 1997*. The Roper Center for Public Opinion Research was also generous in allowing me to select variables from the 1996 General Social Surveys. Sarah Kelbaugh at Allyn and Bacon was a helpful editor.

At the State University of New York at Potsdam, I had the help of my fine colleagues in securing the needed resources and time for this project. I thank SUNY Potsdam's Research and Creative Endeavors Program which provided financial support. The college also provided a course reduction for faculty scholarship. Galen Pletcher and Francis McLaughlin expedited institutional resources in my behalf. David Brouwer, Matthew Keller, and Michael Nuwer adeptly tackled computer-related concerns. I am also indebted to Jackie Rush, Pamela Andrada and Anne True for their professional work in proofreading the text.

I remain indebted to the education I received at the University of New Hampshire. In particular, Cynthia Duncan, Lawrence Hamilton, and Murray Straus provided valuable training which directly related to this project.

I feel gladly compelled to mention my parents, Alfred and Melissa Sweet. My wife and love of my life Jai Rajagopalan has been most supportive and I thank her for the faith in my ability.

Of course any shortcoming in this book is solely my responsibility.

About the Author

Stephen Sweet grew up in the Catskill Mountains of New York. He earned his undergraduate degree in psychology at the State University of New York at Potsdam, before entering into the Peace Corps to teach science in Ghana, West Africa. In between stints at school he also worked as a counselor in a children's home and as a professional carpenter. His master's and doctoral degrees are from the University of New Hampshire. During graduate training he was employed at the *Family Research Lab*, the *Institute for Disability*, and the *Institute for Policy and Social Science Research*. He has done consulting work for the New Hampshire Department of Education, as well as for other private organizations. He has performed research, published articles and presented papers on a variety of subjects including family violence, music, and rural poverty. He is currently an Assistant Professor of Sociology at SUNY Potsdam.

Chapter 1
Key Concepts in Social Science Research

Overview

This chapter examines the major concepts social scientists use to develop research questions and understand data. While you will not be learning about SPSS in this chapter, you will be learning how to approach data from an analytic perspective. This includes constructing testable research questions, selecting indicators, and evaluating causal arguments.

Developing Research Questions

I suspect that if you polled your fellow classmates and asked them why some teenagers drop out of school, you would get a number of plausible ideas. Some likely causes could include overcrowding of classes, insufficient funding for schools, a loss of respect for authority, drugs, boring textbooks, influence of gangs, racial discrimination, and so on. This illustrates that we all have theories which we use to explain patterns of social behavior. Indeed, symbolic interactionist theory points out that without our constant theory making we would be unlikely to create meaningful social encounters at all (Blumer 1969). What distinguishes professionally engaged social science researchers is the degree of formality with which they formulate their research questions and the rigor with which they expose their theories to systematic study.

The initial step in any research project is to identify the **research question**. The research question is what we hope to answer as a result of our study. While this seems straightforward enough, its importance can not be overstated. The research question involves taking some issue, the answer to which many people take for granted, and posing it in a question form so that our research allows us to learn more about the issue. It is the question which drives social science inquiry, not the desire to prove a point.

As a point of illustration, let's examine what happens if a research project is not framed around a solidly framed research question. Suppose that I believe in the science of "numerology" and believe that numbers rule the world. The most grand number of all, I believe, is the number 3. If I (incorrectly) frame my research question as "I want to show the power of the number 3 in the social world," I could find lots of evidence to demonstrate this fact. I may first show the power of 3 in mathematical relations: 24 is divisible by 3, but add 3 to it and one gets 27, which is 3 cubed. Add the digits 2 and 4 (24) and one gets 6, which is divisible by 3! This then explains why there is a Holy Trinity, why clovers have 3 leaves, and why I teach 3 credit classes: it is because 3 is all powerful! According to the semiotician Umberto Eco (1989) this type of logic was not unusual prior to the 16th century.

Scientific reasoning is based on a more skeptical approach to data analysis. Social scientists pose questions so that results contrary to those expected can emerge and be seriously considered. A good research question is very clear in delineating the focus of study and can be framed in a set of testable propositions. "Does the education system foster racial discrimination?" is a much better way to pose a research project than "I want to show that there is discrimination in the education system." When the research project is posed as a question it enables the researcher to focus on a clear analytic strategy. It will also spark a more refined number of subquestions, each of which can be analyzed using different research strategies. For example:

Is there an equitable representation of minority groups within the curriculum?

Is there proportionate employment of minority members in school systems?

To what extent do graduation rates vary among minority groups?

How does funding for schools in minority school districts compare with school
districts in predominantly white areas?

Research questions are best formed in relationship to a **literature review**. The literature review is an overview of the current research concerning a specific topic. Often a project will start out with a vaguely defined research question, which will be refined during the literature review. The best sources for literature reviews will be scholarly journals such as *The American Journal of Sociology*, *Journal of Marriage and the Family*, and *Journal of Social Psychology*, to name but a few. Most articles in scholarly journals have a detailed description of how data were collected and offer extensive references to other related studies. These sources can be obtained by using key word searches of computer data bases located in university libraries.

Theory and Hypothesis

Finding answers to research questions involves developing theories and hypotheses. A **theory** provides an overarching explanation to patterns revealed in the data analysis. According to traditional scientific canons, a theory is something to be tested through hypothesis tests. **Hypotheses** are falsifiable predictions concerning expected relationships. Hypotheses are structured in anticipation that they will be supported when exposed to some type of test. They are also structured in such a way that when the test is performed, unexpected results can potentially occur and the hypotheses will not necessarily be supported. Social scientists tend to place greater faith in the study of empirical data than on unsupported preexisting notions.

Many social scientists use the **deductive approach**, where they set out with a theory and develop a number of hypotheses to be tested. For example, I might theorize that bias in the curriculum may play a big role in influencing the educational attainment of minority groups. The theory, at this point, is only modestly developed. I now can develop some expectations concerning what is expected to be occurring in schools and have some idea of the types of data I should be seeking. Two reasonable hypotheses may be:

Ho 1: Whites will be represented disproportionately in comparison to blacks
         in history textbook pictures.

Ho 2: There will be disproportionately more references to Anglo Saxon Protestant
         names than Hispanic names in history textbook indexes.

Note that each hypothesis is posed in such a way so that it is both testable and falsifiable. Falsifiability is important because it allows unexpected findings to emerge and our expectations to be challenged in the light of critical observation.

It is also important to acknowledge that the deductive approach is not the only approach to data analysis, and that some social scientists suggest that data analysis can also follow a more **inductive approach** termed **grounded theory** (Glaser and Straus 1967). Grounded theory, like traditional deductive social research, relies upon hypotheses, indicators, and well-formed research questions. However, unlike the traditional deductive approach, data are used to develop tentative theories and researchers continually refine the theory to coincide with observations of the data. The research project ends when the researchers understand the relationships found in the data and develop a theory which does as good a job as possible in explaining these relationships. **Exploratory data analysis** is similar in intent (Hoaglin, Mosteller, and Tukey 1983). Advocates suggest that prior to running advanced statistical procedures for the critical test of a hypothesis, researchers should get involved with the data and explore relationships using highly visual depictions of relationships (this will be examined in Chapter 5).

Which is better, the more traditional deductive approach or the inductive approach? I don't think that one is necessarily superior to the other, nor do I think they are independent of one another as is often supposed. I think that good researchers are clear in their logic and develop clear and testable hypotheses. Good researchers also pick their sources of data carefully, know their data sets inside and out, and use their knowledge of the data to build and test theories.

Indicators

Testing hypotheses necessarily involves finding indicators. **Indicators** are observations which make the abstract concept evident and open to measurement. In the above hypotheses, the abstract concept we are trying to examine is bias in the curriculum and two of our indicators are pictures and names used in history textbooks. They serve us well because they are quantifiable and are possible to code into a computer program such as SPSS. Researchers can use any number of indicators. For example, economic prosperity can be indicated by the gross national product (GNP), the per capita income, and even by the number of radios owned per person. Educational success could be indicated by graduation rates, SAT scores, and percentages of young adults attending college. Good indicators should be both reliable and valid.

Reliability refers to the indicator being a consistent measuring device. Some indicators are more consistent than others and the greater consistency the greater reliability of the measuring tool. This is why a metal tape measure estimates distance better than string and why compasses work better for navigation than star gazing. The same concerns extend to social research. In developing our indicators, we strive to select the most consistent tools for measuring concepts such as alienation, alcohol consumption, and depression. A reliable indicator will give the same results if used on repeated occasions. Consider how reliable an indicator would be that relies on counting African American names in history textbooks to measure bias in the curriculum. It probably would not be very reliable because it is often difficult to distinguish African American names from non-African American names. For example, many Americans would not be able to identify W.E.B. Du Bois and William Julius Wilson as African American scholars simply by reading their names. Although far from perfectly reliable, the count of Hispanic names in the index would probably prove much more reliable in determining the degree of representation Hispanics have in the curriculum.

Validity refers to the indicator measuring what it is supposed to measure. One doesn't use a steel ruler to measure temperature because it was never designed to measure heat or cold, and therefore would not be a valid measure. Likewise, a student's grade in a course is not necessarily a valid measure of that student's intelligence. In all likelihood counting the number of pictures of minorities in textbooks would probably be a reasonable way of measuring minority representation in the curriculum, in that it would be quite consistent (reliability) and measure the very thing that we are concerned with (validity).

Variables

All indicators are variables. A **variable** is anything that varies (hence the name). For instance, Mississippi and New York have different high school graduation rates and therefore graduation rates constitute a variable. Other variables include temperature readings, the amount of nicotine in cigarettes, per capita income, and so on.

For now, we will distinguish between two different types of variables, **independent variables** and **dependent variables**. The independent variables are hypothesized to cause changes in dependent variables. In the illustration we have been using, our overarching theory is that preexisting prejudice and racial discrimination result in a biased curriculum. In this case, prejudice constitutes the independent variable and biased curriculum is the dependent variable. This can also be depicted in a simple causal diagram:

Independent Variable   →   Dependent Variable
Racial Discrimination   →   Biased Curriculum

The very same indicators can switch from being independent variables to dependent variables, depending upon the research question being addressed. The way we have phrased the research question to this point has centered around factors influencing the curriculum. The curriculum can in turn have an effect on other factors (such as minority graduation rates), and when analyzed in this way, the curriculum then becomes the independent variable.

Independent Variable   →   Dependent Variable
Biased Curriculum   →   Minority Graduation Rates

Causality

Understanding the differences between independent and dependent variables is crucial, because establishing causality rests on this distinction. To assert a causal relationship is to assert that changes in the independent variable cause changes in the dependent variable. In practice, researchers should only assert that one factor causes the variation in another variable when they can reasonably satisfy the following three criteria:

1. Correlation   there must be a co-relationship between the variables.
2. Time order   the change in the independent variable must precede the change
                            in the dependent variable .
3. Nonspuriousness   the relationship between two variables is not produced by the
                            effects of a third unmeasured "spurious" factor.

Let me offer one example of the need to use causal arguments with care, drawing from a recent debate concerning the book *The Bell Curve* (1994) by Richard Herrnstein and Charles Murray. The authors of *The Bell Curve* argue that there is a causal relationship between intelligence (as measured by IQ scores) and income. Because the authors found a moderate statistical association between IQ and income, they conclude that intelligence (or lack thereof) is the primary factor which determines (causes) a person to become rich or poor. The authors maintain that the same types of causal relationships hold for crime (low IQ causes people to engage in crime) and family structure (low IQ causes people to become single parents). The authors also evoked significant controversy by asserting that race causes intelligence, finding that American whites had a mean IQ of approximately 105 and blacks had an average IQ of approximately 85. In essence, *The Bell Curve* argues that racial minorities do poorly in school and in the workforce because they lack the intellectual ability to do well.

The Bell Curve Thesis

Race and IQ

Independent Variable   Dependent Variable
        Race   →   IQ

IQ and Success

Independent Variable   Dependent Variable
            IQ   →   Educational Success
            IQ   →   Economic Success
            IQ   →   Crime

The Full Causal Model

Race   →   IQ   →   Educational Success
Race   →   IQ   →   Economic Success
Race   →   IQ   →   Crime

The Bell Curve produced a firestorm of criticism (see Fraser 1995). One major concern centered on whether IQ is a valid measure of intelligence. This is a questionable proposition, in that some scholars of intelligence argue that a single measure of intelligence is not altogether valid because people have multiple types of intelligences (Gardiner 1983). However, if we accept the authors' contention that IQ and intelligence are equivalent, can we conclude that a group's low IQ is a strong causal factor in influencing a group's lower placement in the class structure, their comparative lack of success in school, and their comparatively high propensity to commit crime? To establish causality, researchers must satisfy the three criteria for causality listed above: correlation, time order, and nonspuriousness.

To establish the causal relationship, Herrnstein and Murray had to first establish the existence of a **statistical relationship** between IQ and their dependent variables of income, family structure, and crime. A **correlation** means that one variable co-relates with another variable. Because the authors were able to show consistent statistically significant associations (see chapter 4), they were able to satisfy this criterion. One concern leveled by critics of *The Bell Curve* is that the authors imply that their correlations are stronger than the data indicate. The correlations of education, crime, and economic success to IQ were of a magnitude which most researchers would consider as moderate. Whereas *The Bell Curve* suggests that IQ is the primary cause of social success and social pathology, a more critical reading of the moderate correlation between variables indicates that IQ is, at best, only one variable among many other variables which influence success in life.

The authors have much greater difficulties in sustaining criticism relating to the **time order** issue. Researchers claiming that one variable causes changes in another variable must be able to demonstrate in a reasonable way that the independent variable precedes the dependent variable in time. To use some straightforward examples, it is illogical to assume that the illumination of light bulbs is the thing which prompts me to hit a switch in a dark room. It is illogical to assume that catching a fish caused me to put a worm on my line. In both cases the hitting of the light switch and the putting the worm on the line must precede in time the consequences of lighting a room and catching a fish. In relationship to the IQ question, one must ask if the authors have put the cart before the horse.

It might be intuitively appealing to assume that intelligence causes one's success in life, but it is also possible that a person coming from a successful family will have a greater chance of forming a high IQ. Children from wealthier families tend to receive better prenatal care, better nutrition, live in safer environments, and attend better schools. All of these things have a direct impact on a child's IQ. Therefore, being economically privileged may be the factor which causes a person's IQ to become high, not the other way around. The authors of *The Bell Curve* have been less than successful in countering criticisms relating to time order issues.

An Alternative Causal Possibility

Parent's Economic Success   ➔   Child's IQ

The final criterion which *The Bell Curve* must satisfy to establish causality is nonspuriousness. A **spurious relationship** exists when two variables appear to be causally related, but that relationship is caused by the presence of a third unmeasured variable. In spurious relationships, if the third unmeasured variable is taken into account, the relationship between the initial two variables disappears. A classic example of a spurious relationship is that of ice cream appearing to cause drowning deaths. There is a correlation between ice cream and drowning (more people drown during times when a lot of ice cream is being consumed). The time order issue can also be satisfied (increases in ice cream sales precede increases in drowning deaths). Of course the unmeasured factor in this relationship is temperature. More people swim in the summer and more ice cream is consumed in the summer. It is in fact the warm weather operating as a spurious factor, causing both variables to increase.

In the case of race and IQ, *The Bell Curve* effectively establishes both correlation and time order (African Americans, as a group, score lower on IQ tests and a person's race is determined before he or she can perform an IQ test). However, the authors have been severely criticized for not accounting for the possibility of this being a spurious relationship. Blacks disproportionately come from poor families, are more likely to attend inferior schools, and experience a variety of other discriminatory practices relating to physical and social well-being. *The Bell Curve* does not take into account the effects of these factors and therefore leaves open the strong possibility that the findings regarding race and IQ are spurious rather than causal. In fact, research by Thomas Sowell (1978) suggests that once factors such as racial discrimination are taken into account, ethnic and racial differences in IQ largely disappear. In other words, race seems to be associated with IQ, but it is really racial discrimination which produces this apparent relationship.

The Bell Curve Thesis

Black Race   ➔   Low IQ   ➔   Low Socioeconomic Attainment

<u>Possible Spurious Relationship</u>

↗ IQ

Racial Discrimination

↘ Socioeconomic Attainment

The Bell Curve debate illustrates the need to take the issue of causality very seriously before making a hasty conclusion about one variable causing another variable to change. From the debate, we learn that a statistical association or correlation between variables is not sufficient to establish causality. We also learn the need to seriously study the strength of any correlation between variables before we assert that any particular variable is the chief cause of changes in another variable. The time order issue reveals itself to be more complicated than one might initially presuppose. This issue is especially problematic when we make causal arguments based on cross sectional data, which essentially give a snapshot image of social relations at a single point in time. Given the difficulties of measuring social behavior over time, researchers must often use logic to substantiate time order, inferring time order even when it is not possible to empirically establish these claims.

Spuriousness is even more difficult to rule out, simply because it is impossible to account for all potential variables which could produce the appearance of a causal relationship. In actual practice, good research involves measuring those factors which are theoretically likely to produce a spurious relationship. For example, even though sun spots *might* have an effect on the behavior we are interested in studying, because there is no theoretical reason for this assumption we do not account for this in our analysis. However, because factors such as income and education may have a profound impact on social behavior, we take these factors into account just in case they may produce spurious findings while measuring relationships between other variables. In Chapter 6 you will learn more about controlling for spurious factors.

Data Sets

In order to test relationships, researchers must develop **data sets**. Data sets combine variables in such a way that relationships can be tested. Developing data sets to test hypotheses can be one of the most time-consuming parts of a research project. In this text, I have provided a number of indicators at the state level which will enable you to develop and tackle many interesting research questions. In this text package, two data sets are included on disk: the STATES.SAV data and the GSS96.SAV data.

The STATES.SAV data contains **state level data** which describe the characteristics of places. In this data set, each state comprises an observation. For example, you will be able to compare the graduation rates of New York with Kentucky. By looking at the characteristics of places and the experiences of people in each place, we can gain valuable insight into how social forces influence behavior. For example, if we find a positive statistical relationship between education expenditures and graduation rates, state level data will enable us to make pretty strong conclusions concerning the effectiveness of financial support of schooling. There are limitations to state level data, however, which must be acknowledged.

Because the data describe states as a whole, we will not be able to track the experiences of individual people with the STATES.SAV data. Occasionally, researchers forget this and commit an **ecological fallacy**. An ecological fallacy occurs when a researcher makes assertions about the behaviors of individuals on the basis of aggregate measures. Suppose, for example, that I find a place which has high levels of racism and high levels of suicide. I would be wrong to conclude that the people committing suicide did so because they fell victim to racism. I cannot do this because I don't know anything about the individual biographies of the people committing suicide. It is possible, for example, that the people committing suicide could have been the racists and not the victims! It is also possible that the relationship is spurious and that neither the racists nor the victims of racism are committing suicide.

The GSS96.SAV data set, drawn from the General Social Surveys of 1996, is of **individual level data**. These data are the product of interviews with 2904 adult respondents, polling each individual on their personal characteristics (e.g., age, sex, race), their behaviors (e.g., hours of watching television per day), and their attitudes (e.g., whether they are in favor of affirmative action). These data are very strong in showing how people vary in their behaviors and opinions. They are limited, however, in detailing how structural factors (such as school funding) may influence a person's biography.

Summary

Social science research is guided by clearly developed research questions. It places a heavy reliance upon systematic observation and analysis, which requires gathering reliable and valid indicators. Establishing causality is often one of the most challenging aspects of social research because researchers often have to draw conclusions based on cross sectional data. However, rising to the challenge of working with data concerning social behavior is often one of the most rewarding aspects of research.

Key Terms

research question	theory	hypothesis
indicators	reliability	validity
independent variable	dependent variable	causality
correlation	time order	deductive approach
inductive approach	spurious relationship	grounded theory
ecological fallacy	exploratory data analysis	state level data
individual level data		

References and Further Reading

Babbie, Earl. 1998. *The Practice of Social Research, 8 th Edition.* Boston: Wadsworth.

Blumer, Herbert. 1969. *Symbolic Interactionism: Perspective and Method.* Englewood Cliffs, New Jersey: Prentice-Hall.

Eco, Umberto. 1989. *Foucault's Pendulum.* San Diego: Harcourt Brace Jovanovich.

Fraser, Steven. 1995. *The Bell Curve Wars: Race, Intelligence, and the Future of America*. New York: Basic Books.

Gardner, Howard. 1983. *Frames of Mind: Theory of Multiple Intelligences*. New York: Basic Books.

Glaser, Barney and Anselm Straus. 1967. *The Discovery of Grounded Theory*. Chicago: Aldine.

Herrnstein, Richard and Charles Murray. 1994. *The Bell Curve*. New York: Free Press.

Hoaglin, David; Frederick Mosteller, John W. Tukey. 1983. *Understanding Robust and Exploratory Data Analysis*. New York: Wiley.

Neuman, W. Lawrence. 1997. *Social Research Methods: Qualitative and Quantitative Approaches*. Boston: Allyn and Bacon

Sowell, Thomas. 1978. *Essays and Data on American Ethnic Groups*. Washington, DC: The Urban Institute.

U.S. Department of Commerce. 1994. *Statistical Abstract of the United States*. Washington, DC: U.S. Government Printing Office.

Chapter 1 Exercises

Name_____   Date_____

1. Identify the independent and dependent variables in the following research projects:

A.   A study seeks to find out if listening to heavy metal music causes teenagers to become more violent than their peers who do not listen to heavy metal music.

_____   ➔   _____

Independent Variable   Dependent Variable

B.   A group of researchers are interested in examining the effects of long term poverty. They do this by studying subjects' physiological health and attachment to the workforce.

_____   ➔   _____

Independent Variable   Dependent Variable

_____   ➔   _____

Independent Variable   Dependent Variable

C.   A study finds that self-esteem increases as a consequence of receiving good grades on examinations.

_____   ➔   _____

Independent Variable   Dependent Variable

2. Indicators are used to measure abstract concepts. List some indicators which might prove to be reliable and valid in measuring the following concepts:

     A. Economic Prosperity   E.g., Gross National Product

                                        _____

                                        _____

     B. Family Violence   E.g., Admissions to Battered Women's Shelters

                                        _____

                                        _____

     C. Educational Attainment   _____

                                        _____

                                        _____

     D. Religious Commitment   _____

                                        _____

                                        _____

     E. Health   _____

                                        _____

                                        _____

F. Criminality

_____

_____

_____

3. Can you identify a potential spurious factor which may call the following findings into question? Explain.

> Researchers have found a consistent relationship between schools and crime. More crimes occur in neighborhoods surrounding high schools and junior high schools than in neighborhoods far away from schools. The researchers conclude that schools cause crime to occur and believe that this relationship may have something to do with teachers not teaching students the appropriate lessons in the classroom.

4. The U.S. Department of Justice has found that of the children killed by their parents, 55% of the murders were performed by the child's mother and 45% of the murders were performed by the child's father. A researcher uses these data to support his contention that women are more violent than men. On the basis of these data do you find this argument compelling? Why or why not?

5. A social commentator argues that the welfare programs introduced in the 1960s have caused an unparalleled expansion of poverty in the United States. Based on the following data from the *Statistical Abstract of the United States 1994*, would you agree or disagree with this causal statement? Explain.

Year	Percent Below Poverty Level
1960	22%
1965	15%
1970	13%
1975	12%
1980	13%
1985	14%
1990	14%

Chapter 2
Getting Started: Accessing, Examining, and Saving Data

Overview

    This chapter will introduce you to SPSS and the data on your disk. When you complete the exercises in this chapter, you will know how to access the information stored on disk and evaluate the indicators included with this text.

    I suggest that you work through the chapters in this book with the SPSS program running on your computer. As I describe the computer applications, try these commands on your computer. Feel free to explore, as mistakes are never fatal (assuming you remember to save and back up your files - always a good practice!). The chapter will conclude with some guided exercises and you will be asked to perform some of the operations outlined here.

The Layout of SPSS

    When you first start up the SPSS program, you will observe that the program automatically opens to the **SPSS Data Editor Window**. This screen looks very much like a spreadsheet, and in fact operates on similar principles as spreadsheet programs. Because there are no data in the SPSS program when you initially start the program, the grid is empty and the Data Editor Window says "Untitled." Your screen should look like Figure 2.1.

    SPSS for Windows is menu driven, meaning that the program is designed to fulfill the most common requests and offers a quick path to getting those requests filled. There are two types of menus located at the top of this window. The **menu bar** contains an organized path to find the most commonly requested procedures involving opening files, performing statistical operations, and constructing graphs. As we work through the SPSS program, you will learn many of the commands made possible through the menu bar. You can start exploring some of these capacities by using the mouse to draw the cursor to a command category, such as *File* (Figure 2.2) or *Statistics* (Figure 2.3), hold down the left mouse button, and examine the operations which fall under each of these command subjects.

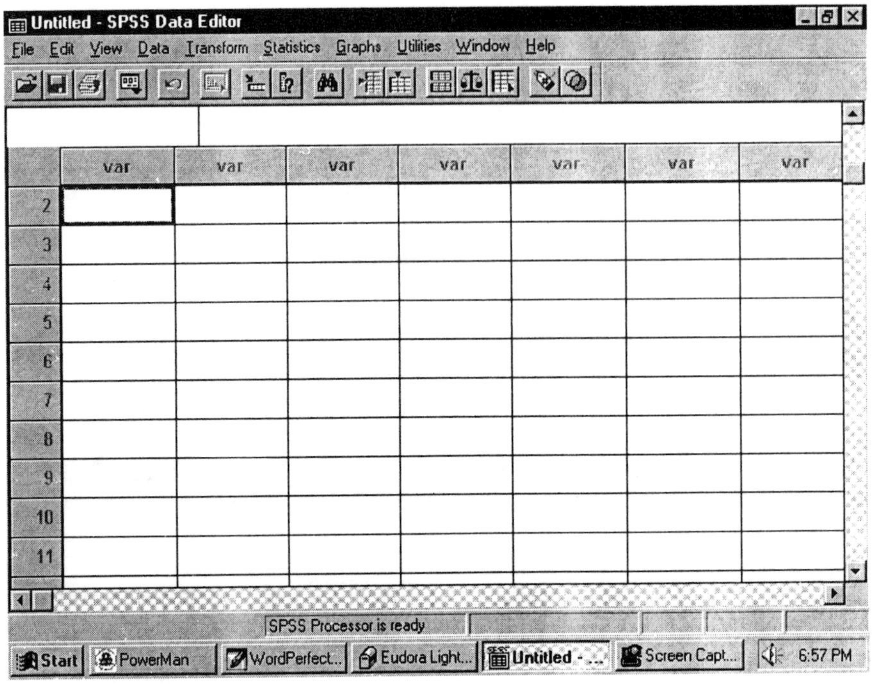

Figure 2.1 The Data Editor Window

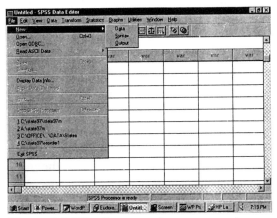

Figure 2.2 File Commands

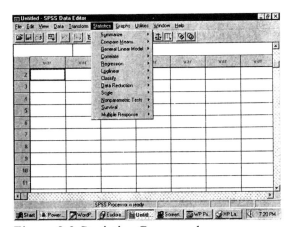

Figure 2.3 Statistics Commands

If you want to do a particular command (don't do this now) continue to hold the mouse button down, move the cursor to the command which you wish to perform, release the button, and the program will ask you for specific information needed to perform that command.

In this text, I will be using a shorthand method of describing how to locate specific commands. For instance, if I want you to open a new data file, you will see the following:

File

   New

      Data

This is a shorthand way of saying: go to the *File* command from the main menu, hold down the mouse button, move the cursor to highlight *New,* and then move the cursor to highlight *Data.* Upon releasing the mouse button, you will have told the computer to open a new data file and SPSS will give you a format from which to enter the pertinent information.

Beneath the menu bar is the **tool bar**. This works like the menu and by pointing and clicking the mouse you will be able to use a number of handy devices to refine the presentation of your data. We will not worry too much about using the tool bar, but as you become more familiar with the program you will probably find yourself curious as to what types of things the tool bar can do. Feel free to experiment.

Not incidentally, there is another way to run command procedures in SPSS by using **syntax commands**. Unlike the menu driven procedures, syntax commands require a greater familiarity with the particular terminology and phrasing necessary for SPSS to perform statistical procedures. It is likely that your professor first learned to use SPSS on earlier versions of the program, which relied exclusively on these syntax commands. For complex and repetitive procedures, this is still probably the most efficient way to work with SPSS (this was the way in which I constructed the data sets included in your package). However, for the purposes of the current activities, you will probably be served well by concentrating solely on the menu commands.

Defining and Saving a New Data Set

The first step in analyzing data involves loading a data set into the statistical package. This can be done in two ways: inputting data manually to create a new data set or by accessing an already constructed data set.

Inputting a new data set is the first step in a research project following the initial collection of data. It is also a good way to get a feel for the structure of the SPSS program and how the system operates. In this exercise you will learn the fundamental processes involved in constructing a new data set. To illustrate the process we will generate a data set concerning your family members. Your data set will contain four variables: Name, Sex, Birth Date, and Education. Each family member will constitute one case in the data set. In the event that your family is very small, you could also include friends or other relatives.

To define the variables in your data set, click the cursor onto the first column of the *Data Editor* window, and then from the *Data* menu, select *Define Variable*. The *Define Variable* function specifies the ways in which SPSS will deal with the information you will enter. Enter "NAME" as the *Variable Name.* Click on *Labels* and enter "Family Member Name" as the *Variable Label.* Click on *Type* and enter "20" in the box for *Characters*. This informs SPSS that this variable can be up to 20 characters long and that the information can be treated as written text rather than as numerical data. Using our shorthand method, these commands are represented as:

> *Data*
> > *Define*
> > > *Variable Name*: NAME
> > > > *Labels*
> > > > > *Variable Label*: Family Member Name
> > > > *Type*
> > > > > *Type*: String
> > > > > *Characters*: 20

 Click OK to continue and you will observe that a new window appears, the **SPSS Output Navigator** window (Figure 2.4).

This *Output Navigator* window displays the output from the commands you just entered in the form of SPSS syntax commands. As you continue to work through the menu commands, you will begin to learn SPSS syntax by observing this output. For our purposes, however, using the menus will be sufficient. You can click on the X in the upper right hand corner of this output and respond "No," that you do not want to save this output.

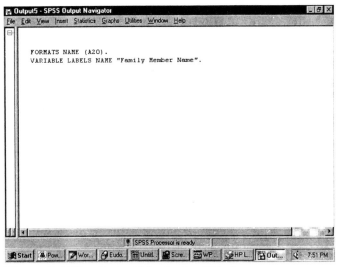

Figure 2.4 The Output Navigator Window

You will see that the *Data Editor* window now has a new variable in the first column called "NAME." In this column you can enter data for each case in your data set, the names of your relatives. Place the cursor in the box intersecting the first column and the first row; click to highlight that box. Enter your own name, and press Enter. In the rows below enter your spouse's, parents', siblings', and childrens' names. Your *Data Editor* window should look similar to Figure 2.5. If names are clipped off, you can expand this row by placing the cursor at the intersection of this column with the next column until the double arrow appears; click and hold the mouse and draw the column to the right.

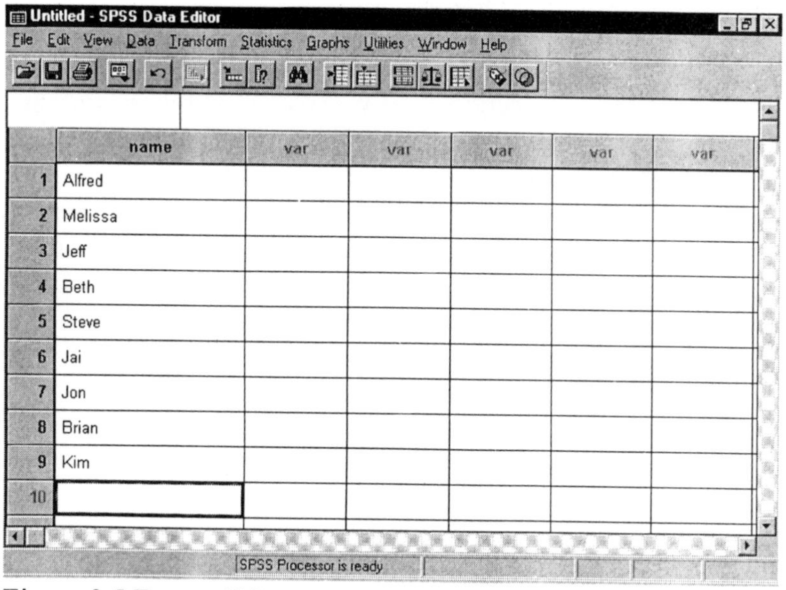

Figure 2.5 Entry of Names with Data Editor

The other variables can be inputted in a similar manner. Move the cursor to the next column in the *Data Editor* window, *define* the next variable as "SEX," *label* it as "sex." We could make this variable a string variable, but in this case we will keep SEX as a numeric variable with a length of 8 characters and 2 decimal places. Represent males with the number "1" and females with the number "2." Within the *Labels* box, enter in the *Value Labels* "1" as the *Value* and "Male" as the *Value Label*, click on *Add*. Do the same for women by entering "2" as the *Value* and "Female" as the *Value Label*. Click on *Add*. Click on *Continue* and click on *OK*. Exit from the Output Navigator Window. Using the shorthand system, these commands are:

Data
>   Define
>   >   Variable Name: SEX
>   >   >   Labels
>   >   >   >   Variable Label: Sex
>   >   >   >   Value: 1
>   >   >   >   Value Label: Male
>   >   >   >   Value: 2
>   >   >   >   Value Label: Female
>   >   >   Type
>   >   >   >   Type: Numeric
>   >   >   >   Width: 8
>   >   >   >   Decimal: 2

You can now enter the appropriate numeric values in the column for the variable SEX in the *Data Editor* window.

Move the cursor to highlight the third column in the *Data Editor* window. Define a new variable for birth date as "BIRTHDT" and *label* the variable "Birth Date." Because we want this to be treated as a date in the data, click on *Type* and select Date. Date offers a number of formats for coding the information, select mm/dd/yy and input the appropriate birth dates from the *Data Editor* window. Again, these commands can be represented in shorthand:

Data
>   Define
>   >   Variable Name: BIRTHDT
>   >   >   Labels
>   >   >   >   Variable Label: Birth Date
>   >   >   Type
>   >   >   >   Type: Date
>   >   >   >   Type: mm/dd/yy.

Highlight the fourth column in the Data Editor window. *Define* a new variable for education as "EDYRS" and *label* the variable "Years of Education." Because SPSS automatically codes this variable as numeric, there is no need to do any further commands. Using the shorthand method:

Data
>   Define
>   >   Variable Name: EDYRS
>   >   >   Labels
>   >   >   >   Variable Label: Years of Education.

When you enter the appropriate values in the *Data Editor* window, your data set should look similar to that represented in Figure 2.6.

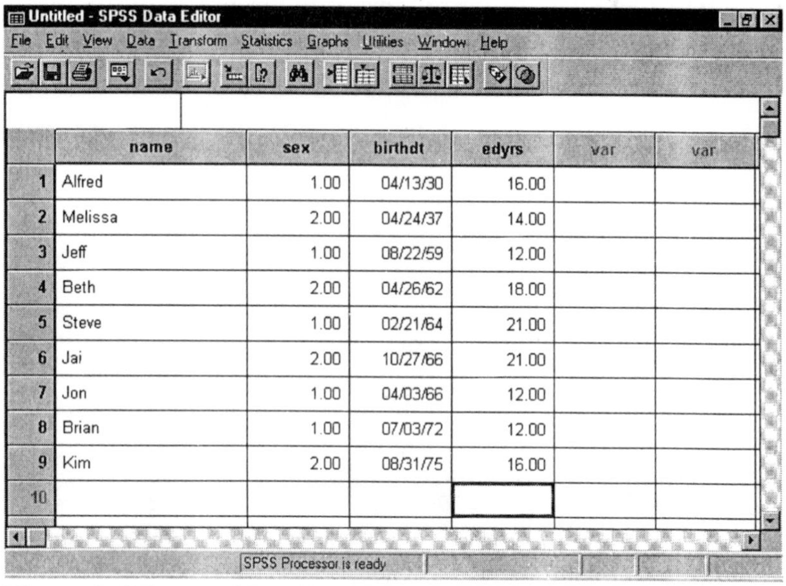

Figure 2.6 Entry of Family Data

In some circumstances researchers lack the necessary information to enter information for a particular case. For example, if I did not know my father's birth date, the most appropriate method of dealing with this problem is to code that as "missing." This is done by entering a period (.) as the value.

We will work with the data you compiled here again in the future. For now, however, save your data using:

File
> *Save As*: FAMILY.SAV.

Save this data on a formatted disk with the name "FAMILY.SAV." I would suggest saving these data on a new disk. Make sure SPSS saves the data to the A drive, using the *Save in:* box located at the top of the window. Congratulations, you have just defined variables, labeled variables, labeled values, and saved your data.

Loading and Examining an Existing File

As you can tell, inputting data can be labor intensive and time consuming. For this reason, many professional social science researchers allot this task to companies that specialize in data entry. Thankfully, much social science research can use data already compiled by government agencies or by other researchers. In fact, on the Internet there are now a number of organizations, such as the Inter-university Consortium for Political and Social Research, which specialize in distributing information ready for analysis. Also, your college library probably has a large quantity of government data in computer ready format.

On the diskette accompanying this text is a data set containing state level data, STATES.SAV. These data are drawn from a number of sources such as the Department of the Census and the FBI. To examine this data set, use:

> *File*
>> *Open*
>>> *Data:* STATES.SAV .

Your computer has to search for these data in the correct place, so make sure that *Look in:* (located at the top of the window) is directed to the A Drive of your computer (Figure 2.7).

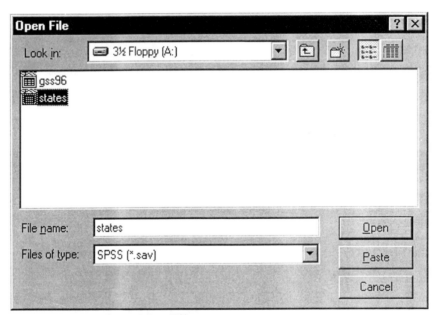

Figure 2.7 Opening a New File

You will see the *Data Editor* window fill with data from the 50 United States and the District of Columbia. Just as your family members comprised cases in the previous exercise, each state comprises a single case in this data set. Your screen should look like Figure 2.8.

st		state	region9	region4	cjc199	cjc202
1	1	ALABAMA	5.00	3.00	3383.60	1417.60
2	2	ALASKA	9.00	4.00	8518.20	3819.40
3	3	ARIZONA	8.00	4.00	14447.30	4040.70
4	4	ARKANSAS	6.00	3.00	6616.60	2173.30
5	5	CALIFORNIA	9.00	4.00	7415.60	2901.80
6	6	COLORADO	8.00	4.00	11972.00	3993.20
7	7	CONNECTICUT	1.00	1.00	11807.80	3693.70
8	8	DELAWARE	4.00	3.00	16499.50	8023.30
9	9	DISTRICT OF COLUMBI	4.00	3.00	9361.50	3722.10
10	10	FLORIDA	4.00	3.00	10279.30	4064.40

Figure 2.8 Data Editor Display of STATES.SAV

There are scores of variables in this data set, such as indicators of population, educational attainment, income, and health care. Each variable is represented by a name, shown across the top row of the *Data Editor* window. One easy way to find the list of all of the variable names and variable labels of numeric data is to use:

Statistics
>*Summarize*
>>*Descriptives*.

You can select any (or all) of the desired variables by highlighting the variables and sending them into the "variables box" by clicking on the arrow in the center of the window.   For now, highlight the first 10 variables (Figure 2.9). When you have done this click on *OK* and you will have performed your first statistical operation in SPSS.

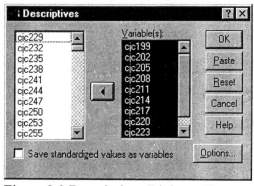

Figure 2.9 Descriptives Dialogue Box

Descriptive Statistics

	N	Minimum	Maximum	Mean	Std. Deviation
CJC199 'Juvenile Arrest Rate 1995'	47	1158.50	22250.90	10052.6	3820.841
CJC202 'Juvenile Arrest Rate:Crime Index Offenses 1995'	47	409.20	8023.30	3268.29	1191.338
CJC205 'Juvenile Arrest Rate:Violent Crime 1995'	47	28.80	1527.60	455.0702	291.0781
CJC208 'Juvenile Arrest Rate:Murder 1995'	47	.00	32.40	10.7511	8.2359
CJC226 'Arrest Rate of Juveniles:Larceny&Theft 1995'	47	181.70	6276.30	2040.76	1035.130
Valid N (listwise)	47				

Figure 2.10 Descriptive Statistics Output

The output from the descriptives will comprise a summary of the variables contained in the data set. The *Descriptives* command displays summary statistics of each variable selected, including the Mean, Standard Deviation, Minimum Value, Maximum Value, and the Valid N (the number of cases), and the Variable Label (Figure 2.10).

In the next chapter we will develop skills in univariate analysis (examining individual variables in isolation from other variables). For the time being we will concentrate on viewing the variable names and the variable labels. Note, however, that the *Descriptives* command gives us plenty of other information. For instance, if I were interested in studying juvenile crime, it is important to know that variable CJC199 signifies the Juvenile Arrest Rate in 1995. In 1995, there was an average of 10052.6 arrests per 100,000 juveniles, the lowest rate of arrest was 1158/100,000, and the highest rate of arrest was 22250/100,000. In the event that your output does not look like that reproduced above, examine the *Options* in the descriptives command and check off the type of output you desire.

Statistics
    Descriptives
        Options

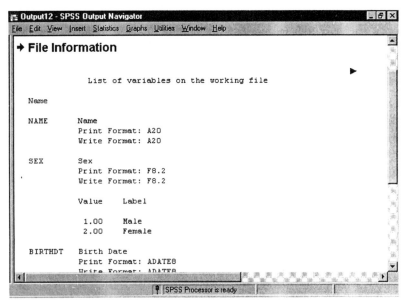

Figure 2.11 File Info of FAMILY.SAV

Another way of learning the variable names and labels in a data set is to use the command:

Utilities
  File Info.

This command will display all of the variable names and labels, as well as yield information on how these variables are defined (e.g., string, numeric, or date). Load in your the data from FAMILY.SAV (the data you previously constructed) and run the *File Info* command. Your output should look similar to that reproduced in Figure 2.11.

Dropping and Adding Variables in the Data Editor

A good data analyst will become skilled at selecting those data which are pertinent to his/her research questions. There is currently so much information available that it is easy to become overwhelmed by having too much rather than too little data. Let's suppose, for the moment, that you are interested in looking at the issue of environmentalism. As you compile data concerning recycling, car pooling, etc., you come across homicide statistics. There might be a relationship between homicide and recycling, but you have to ask yourself at this point, does this new variable have anything to do with my main research question? If it does, keep it in your data set. If it doesn't, there is no reason to keep it in the data because it will only take up disk space and possibly later cloud your thinking about what needs to be analyzed.

There are a number of ways to drop variables from the data. One way is simply to go to the top of the *Data Editor* window, highlight the column of the variable that is not desired, and use the *Edit* command:

> *Edit*
>> *Cut.*

You can try this function by opening your data FAMILY.SAV and cutting the variable EDYRS. You will see this variable disappear from the *Data Editor* window. This variable can be restored by using:

> *Edit*
>> *Undo Cut.*

It is also possible to add a new variable to the data set using the command:

> *Data*
>> *Insert Variable.*

Of course once you insert a new variable, you will need to define the variable and enter the appropriate values in the same manner described earlier in this chapter. It is important to note that any changes to your data (such as adding or deleting variables) will be saved only if you save the data set before exiting the program. If you do not save the data, any changes you have made will be lost. If you make substantial changes to a data set, it is prudent to save that file under a new name. As I work with data, I usually give the initial file a name such as "CRIME1.SAV." As I refine the data, adding or deleting variables, I save the new files with successive new names such as "CRIME2.SAV," "CRIME3.SAV," etc. The advantage of doing this is that it enables me to backtrack and correct any (inevitable) mistakes that I make along the way. You might develop your own system, but recognize that it is important to keep a running record of any changes you make to your data. It is also important to never copy over the original data set unless you are confident that you want all of the changes to remain. Once a data set is copied over, the data are changed forever.

Naming and Labeling Variables

You may have noticed that the data in the STATES data set have names which appear cumbersome. For example, why didn't I just name variable CJC199 (Juvenile Arrest Rate in 1995) JuvenileArrests? Unfortunately SPSS limits variable names to 8 characters or fewer. This means that almost all variables will need truncated names. Because there are so many variables relating to juvenile crime in this data set, I decided to indicate this with the initials CJ (the first two letters in the name) indicating crime:juvenile. The remaining letters and numbers indicate the source of the data. In the case of the STATES data set, all of the data have been drawn from two books:

Crime State Rankings 1997   *State Rankings 1997.*

The third letter in the variable name indicates the source of the data. C= *Crime State Rankings 1997*,

S= *State Rankings 1997.* The remaining numbers indicate the page of the text from which these data were drawn. Using these variable names and these texts, the data can be used to trace the data back to its original sources.

For example, variable CJC199 can be interpreted as:

CJ- Juvenile Crime
C- <u>Crime State Rankings 1997</u>
199- Page 199.

To simplify searches of the data for specific subjects, below is a list of abbreviations used in the variable names in the STATES data.

<u>Variable Name Prefixes</u>
cj - juvenile crime
cr - crime
cp - prisons
dm - demography, population
ee - economy
en - environment
ht - health
jb - employment
pv - poverty
sc - schooling
tx - taxation
vt - voting
ww - defense

On the surface, this may seem a cumbersome approach to naming variables because the names are not intuitively transparent. However, it offers a few advantages because it is systematic and allows the researcher to locate the variables quickly, it groups similar concepts together alphabetically, and enables location of the original source of the data. As you gain experience in working with data, you will develop your own system of labeling data.

SPSS also limits how long variable labels can be. Labels can be up to 120 characters long, but often these labels will be cut off in some of the SPSS output. I generally restrict labels to about 80 characters, so that they can be fully displayed. However, this often necessitates abbreviating words in complicated or lengthy labels. In the STATES data, I have been forced to abbreviate in a number of circumstances. In most cases the abbreviation will be apparent. I have included at the end of this book an appendix of common abbreviations.

Merging and Importing Files

In some circumstances, the data you desire to work with may exist in a form other than SPSS format. All of the data provided with this text are in SPSS format, which makes your work much easier. However, at some point in your career, you may find it necessary to import statistical information from another format, such as Lotus, Excel, dBase, or ASCII. You will find SPSS has the capability of importing this information within the command:

File
>   *Open*
>>   *Data*
>>>   *File Type.*

In compiling the data for your analysis, I accessed a number of different sources of data, and selected those variables which I thought would be most pertinent for the types of research projects students would be interested in performing, and then combined these different sources through a process called merging.

Data
>   *Merge Files*
>>   *Add Variables.*

The above command operates by combining two data sets in such a way that new variables are added on to the end of a primary file. Suppose you had a file containing your family members' social security numbers and wanted to add this information to the data set you compiled earlier. The *Add Variables* command would enable you to do this operation by merging the files according to the selected variables. You would need to first sort both files so that each family member occurs in the same order in each file using the command:

Data
>   *Sort.*

Once each file is ordered in a similar manner, SPSS can match cases so that the appropriate information is added to each case.

It is also possible to append new cases into the data set using the *Merge Files* command. Suppose, for example, that you wanted to combine the information about your family with that compiled by other class members. So long as each file has all of the same variables, new cases (people) can be added using:

Data
>   *Merge Files*
>>   *Add Cases.*

There is no immediate need for you to import files or merge them. However, in the future you may find that you want to add some variables to the data set included with this text or construct an entirely new data set from existing data. If this is the case, you will probably need to use the merge or import procedures.

Summary

In this chapter you learned how to construct a data set and how to retrieve existing data. Data management is a skill which involves selecting appropriate data and developing systematic methods of saving and naming data sets. SPSS has the capacity to import data from other computer programs and to combine data from different sources into a single data set.

Key Terms

SPSS Data Editor	SPSS Output Navigator	descriptives
merging	importing	labeling
syntax commands		

References and Further Reading

Morgan, Kathleen O'Leary, Scott Morgan and Neal Quitno. 1997. *State Rankings 1997.* Lawrence, Kansas: Morgan Quitno.

Morgan, Kathleen O'Leary, Scott Morgan and Neal Quitno. 1997. *Crime State Rankings 1997.* Lawrence, Kansas: Morgan Quitno.

Chapter 2 Exercises

Name_____   Date_____

1. Open your file FAMILY.SAV, run descriptives, and print the results.
   Printing can accomplished by using: *File*
                                                        Print

2. Create a new data set by polling 5 other people and asking the following questions:

   RESPOND. What are the last four digits of your social security number?

   EXER1. Do you exercise regularly? (Yes or No)

   EXER2. How many hours a week would you say you exercise?

   EXER3. Do you participate in team sports? (Yes or No)

   EXER4. What is your favorite sport to play?

   Create a new data set using these data and incorporating the following labels.

Variable Name	Label	Value Labels	Variable Type
RESPOND	Respondent Number	None	Numeric
EXER1	Exercise Regularly?	0=no 1=yes	Numeric
EXER2	Hours/Week of Exercise	None	Numeric
EXER3	Participate in Team Sports?	0=no 1=yes	Numeric
EXER4	Favorite Sport	None	String 20

   Input the responses and save the data as "EXERCISE.SAV". Print *File Info* of all of the variables. Print a copy of the Data Editor window.

3. Open the data STATES.SAV. Examine the data set using the *file info* command and locate some variables which measure the following concepts. Then use the *descriptives* command to find the mean values of these variables:

A. Economic Prosperity

Variable Name	Mean	Variable Label

Variable Name	Mean	Variable Label

Variable Name	Mean	Variable Label

B. Health

Variable Name	Mean	Variable Label

Variable Name	Mean	Variable Label

Variable Name	Mean	Variable Label

C. Education

Variable Name	Mean	Variable Label

Variable Name	Mean	Variable Label

Variable Name	Mean	Variable Label

D. Population

Variable Name	Mean	Variable Label

Variable Name	Mean	Variable Label

Variable Name	Mean	Variable Label

E. Welfare Use

Variable Name	Mean	Variable Label

Variable Name	Mean	Variable Label

Variable Name	Mean	Variable Label

Chapter 3
Univariate Analysis

Overview

Now that you are skilled at accessing data and creating new variables, you are in a good position to start analyzing data through univariate analysis. **Univariate analysis** involves the exploration of the characteristics of any single variable in isolation from other variables in the study. In this chapter you will learn about the major approaches to univariate analysis and the procedures necessary to generate new variables from existing variables.

Most social science research is interested in looking at relationships between variables, such as the relationship between education and crime, income and education, or religion and suicide. If this is the case, then why engage in univariate analysis and study variables in isolation from one another?

Possibly the foremost reason is that univariate analysis is very informative. For example, to fully understand whether education affects crime requires understanding the percent of the population that drops out of high school, the percent that graduates from high school, and the percent that goes on to higher education. If crime is a concern, what are the overall crime rates? If poverty is a major concern, it is necessary to determine the distribution of income in the United States and the proportion of the population that is poor. If we want to understand factors which contribute to out-of-wedlock births, we need to understand how high this rate is in any given year. While the relationship between variables is important, this type of information is essential for understanding the full implications of any study.

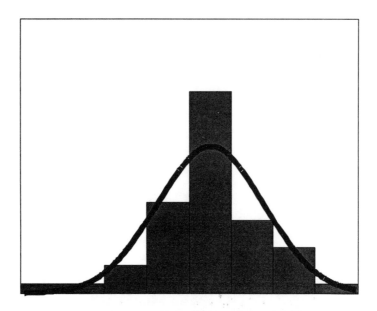

Figure 3.1 Normal Curve Imposed Over a Histogram

A second reason for engaging in univariate analysis involves determining which types of statistical analyses are appropriate to use in bivariate and multivariate procedures. In subsequent chapters, you will learn that advanced statistical procedures rely on assumptions concerning the distribution of data of individual variables. For example, many mean-based statistical procedures, such as regression, rely on variables conforming to a "normal" or "bell-shaped" distribution (Figure 3.1). If the distributions of the variables do not conform to the normal distribution (something that can only be determined through univariate analysis) it may prove necessary to opt for other "non-parametric" statistical procedures.

Sorting Data
You already know one way of examining the data in any particular variable, which is simply to scroll through the information displayed in the *Data Editor* window. As point of illustration, open the data set STATES.SAV. By scrolling down under any particular variable, you can observe the values of the data in any particular variable. Likewise, if you are interested in the values for a particular state, such as New York, you highlight New York and scroll across and examine all of the data for that particular case. This is the most rudimentary way of looking at data and is not so much statistically based as it is just an inspection process. You can impose an order on the data by ranking it from low to high (or high to low) with the *sort* command:

Data
   Sort Cases

To illustrate this procedure, *Sort* the data by variable REGION9 (Census Regions 9). When you do this, you will see that the data in the *Data Editor* window have been rearranged from low value to high value in variable REGION9. The states are now reordered, with New England states grouped together, Mid-Atlantic states grouped together, etc.

    Sort the data again by variable CJC199 (Juvenile Arrest Rate 1995). By doing this, we can rank the states according to this particular variable. Use the following procedure to display the cases in their new sorted order (Figure 3.2):

       Statistics
           Summarize
                Case Summaries
                      Variables: CJC199
                          STATE.

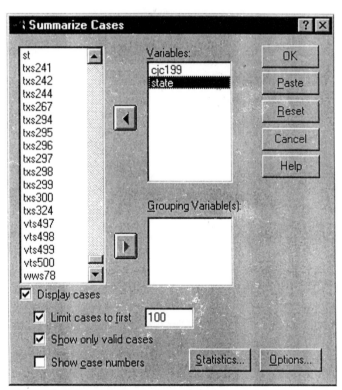

Figure 3.2 Case Summaries Dialogue Box

You should produce output which looks similar to that represented in Figure 3.3. The first four states, New Hampshire, Illinois, Kansas, and Montana, are coded as missing for this particular variable. Vermont has the lowest juvenile arrest rate and Wisconsin has the highest arrest rate. Take a few moments and locate your state's juvenile arrest rate in these data. Where does it rank?

You might want to try the sort function with a few other variables. When you finish, sort the data by variable ST and the data will return to their original order.

Case Summaries [a]

	CJC199 'Juvenile Arrest Rate 1995'	STATE
1	.	ILLINOIS
2	.	KANSAS
3	.	MONTANA
4	.	NEW HAMPSHIRE
5	1158.50	VERMONT
6	3383.60	ALABAMA
7	3709.40	WEST VIRGINIA
8	4791.90	MASSACHUSETTS
9	5888.60	MICHIGAN
10	6034.70	IOWA
11	6530.40	SOUTH CAROLINA
12	6556.00	GEORGIA
13	6616.60	ARKANSAS
14	7081.00	NORTH CAROLINA
15	7294.50	OKLAHOMA
16	7415.60	CALIFORNIA
17	7951.00	VIRGINIA
18	8034.20	MAINE
19	8518.20	ALASKA
20	8653.20	MISSISSIPPI
21	9013.30	KENTUCKY
22	9150.60	NEW YORK
23	9269.70	NEBRASKA
24	9295.40	MARYLAND
25	9361.50	DISTRICT OF COLUMBIA
26	9586.70	RHODE ISLAND
27	9781.40	MISSOURI
28	9819.10	LOUISIANA
29	9821.70	TEXAS
30	10120.80	WASHINGTON
31	10206.70	INDIANA
32	10279.30	FLORIDA
33	10282.50	TENNESSEE
34	10504.70	OHIO
35	11273.70	WYOMING
36	11283.20	NEW JERSEY
37	11807.80	CONNECTICUT
38	11809.00	PENNSYLVANIA
39	11972.00	COLORADO
40	12217.20	MINNESOTA
41	12265.80	NEVADA
42	12750.60	NORTH DAKOTA
43	13559.80	UTAH
44	13811.70	OREGON
45	14447.30	ARIZONA
46	14538.50	IDAHO
47	14558.20	HAWAII
48	15133.70	NEW MEXICO
49	16182.90	SOUTH DAKOTA
50	16499.50	DELAWARE
51	22250.90	WISCONSIN
Total N	47	51

a. Limited to first 100 cases.

Figure 3.3 Juvenile Arrest Rates 1995

Measures of Central Tendency

Examining data through the *Data Editor* window can be useful in some circumstances, especially when looking at data to detect specific values by case or to identify sources of error in the data. The larger the data set, however, the more difficult it becomes to glean meaning from the data using this method. For this reason, much univariate analysis relies upon determining a **measure of central tendency** for a variable. There are various ways of measuring the central tendency of a particular variable, but all share one thing in common: they are an attempt to determine that point at which the data are centered. If we can find the location of central tendency, we can obtain a good sense of the midpoint of the data. The measure of central tendency is used to give us an understanding of the "average" or "typical" case. The use of the word "average," however, is not altogether accurate because it implies a mathematical average and ignores other common measures of central tendency such as the median and the mode.

One way of determining central tendency is to locate the **mode**, the most frequently recorded value in any variable. Of the three measures of central tendency, the mode is probably the least often relied upon statistic. There are times, however, where the mode can be a highly useful piece of information. Consider if we wanted to describe the criminal behavior of individual juvenile delinquents. Juvenile delinquents vary in how often they commit crimes and there are likely to be many differences in the case histories of individual kids. However, if we could describe the most commonly reported number of criminal acts engaged in by each kid (the mode number of crimes), we may have a fairly good understanding of the frequency of criminal behaviors of the "typical" juvenile delinquent. This would be especially important if a few "hard core" delinquents engage in hundreds of acts of crime per year and most delinquents only engage in one or two acts per year. If we did not know the mode, we might conclude that most delinquents engage in higher numbers of crimes per year than is actually typical of most of the kids in the group.

The mode of any continuous variable can be determined in SPSS by using the frequencies command:

> *Statistics*
> *Frequencies.*

The *Frequencies* command displays the number of times each value of the data is observed in a particular variable. As point of illustration, generate a frequency distribution using the variable CPC77 (Prisoners Executed 1977-95) (Figure 3.4).

The mode for this particular variable is 0, indicating that 25 states (49%) executed no prisoners during this time period. The next most common number of executions was 1 person, the number of executions performed by 5 states (9.8%), as observed in the Frequency column. These data seem to indicate that executions are not very common social experiences. However, there is one state which executed 104 prisoners. Perhaps you can guess which state this is. See if you were correct using *Sort* then *Case Summaries*.

Frequencies

CPC77 'Prisoners Executed:1977-95'

		Frequency	Percent	Valid Percent	Cumulative Percent
Valid	.00	25	49.0	49.0	49.0
	1.00	5	9.8	9.8	58.8
	2.00	3	5.9	5.9	64.7
	3.00	1	2.0	2.0	66.7
	4.00	3	5.9	5.9	72.5
	5.00	3	5.9	5.9	78.4
	6.00	1	2.0	2.0	80.4
	7.00	1	2.0	2.0	82.4
	8.00	1	2.0	2.0	84.3
	11.00	1	2.0	2.0	86.3
	12.00	1	2.0	2.0	88.2
	17.00	1	2.0	2.0	90.2
	20.00	1	2.0	2.0	92.2
	22.00	1	2.0	2.0	94.1
	29.00	1	2.0	2.0	96.1
	36.00	1	2.0	2.0	98.0
	104.00	1	2.0	2.0	100.0
	Total	51	100.0	100.0	
Total		51	100.0		

Figure 3.4 Frequency Output of Variable CPC77

The mean is generally what people refer to when they say "average." In all likelihood, your grade point average (GPA) is calculated using a variation on the above formula, whereby your college averages together the outcome of all of your courses (all of which may be weighted differently in the final calculation). This will ultimately produce your mean GPA, which is the indicator of the central tendency of all of your work. For data analysts, the **mean** constitutes the measure of central tendency as determined by the mathematical average.

$$\text{MEAN} = \frac{\text{SUM OF THE VALUES OF ALL CASES}}{\text{TOTAL NUMBER OF CASES}}$$

The mean is probably the most commonly used statistic by social scientists. It is especially useful when discussing research findings with the general public who are less likely to be conversant in interpreting more advanced statistics such as regression coefficients. For example, newspaper reports of average SAT scores almost always refer to the mean SAT scores of all students. Many of the indicators in your data sets are based upon means, such as the average amount spent per pupil in each state. Another reason why the mean is important is that it is the basis of many of the "**parametric**" or "**mean-based**" statistical procedures such as ordinary least squares regression or analysis of variance (ANOVA), which are used to examine relationships between variables. It is important to note that all parametric (mean-based) statistical procedures assume that the distribution of the data follows the distribution of the normal curve. When the data appear "normal," the mean is a good measure of central tendency. The more skewed or non-normal the distribution, the less faith can be placed upon the mean as a valid indicator of central tendency.

You have already found one way of locating the mean, by using the *Descriptives* command:

> *Statistics*
> > *Summarize*
> > > *Descriptives.*

Locate the mean of variable CPC77 (Prisoners Executed 1977-95) using the *Descriptives* command. You should find the mean number of executions to be 6.13. Now think about the purpose of a measure of central tendency, which is to generate a value which indicates the most typical observation. Which do you think works better at indicating the typical number of executions per state, the mode (0 executions) or the mean (6.13 executions)? The answer is not necessarily clear cut, but in this case I would bend towards the mode rather than the mean. One reason is that Texas, because it has such a high rate of executions, tends to pull the mean to a value which is higher than accurately reflects the number of executions in most states.

The **median** is intended to signify that point in the data that separates the upper 50% of the cases from the lower 50% of the cases. As a measure of central tendency, the median is a useful statistic, especially when the data are strongly skewed. Income, for instance, is a strongly skewed variable in that there is a small select subpopulation that receives a disproportionate amount of the income earned in any given year (e.g., Bill Gates and Oprah Winfrey). Gilbert and Kahl (1993) estimate that the top 5% of households received approximately 25% of the total income distributed in 1990. If we used the mean to determine the "average" or "typical" income of American households, the "average" American household would appear to be earning about $41,369. This is $9,000 more than the median household income of $32,142.

A way of finding both the median and the mean of a variable is to use the SPSS *Explore* command:

> *Statistics*
> > *Summarize*
> > > *Explore.*

Take a few minutes and put this into practice. Generate *Explore* output for variable CPC77 (place CPC77 in the *Dependent Variable* box in the *Explore* window). Your output should look similar to that displayed in Figure 3.5.

Descriptives

			Statistic	Std. Error
CPC77 'Prisoners Executed:1977-95'	Mean		6.1373	2.2376
	95% Confidence Interval for Mean	Lower Bound	1.6428	
		Upper Bound	10.6317	
	5% Trimmed Mean		3.4216	
	Median		1.0000	
	Variance		255.361	
	Std. Deviation		15.9800	
	Minimum		.00	
	Maximum		104.00	
	Range		104.00	
	Interquartile Range		5.0000	
	Skewness		4.986	.333
	Kurtosis		28.954	.656

Figure 3.5 Descriptives Output for Variable CPC77

Here we find the median value for CPC77 is 1. This indicates that the "typical" state, as indicated by the median, had one execution from 1977-1995. Again, consider if this seems a more accurate assessment than the mode or mean measure of central tendency. In my opinion, I think the median works quite well for this variable. Because the median operates by locating the point at which 50% of state executions fall above and 50% of state executions fall below, the influence of Texas no longer has such a dramatic influence in determining our estimate of the location of central tendency. At the same time, the fact that 51% of the states have had at least one execution over this time period seems to call into question the validity of the mode (0) as an appropriate measure of central tendency.

From the above discussion, you might already understand why sometimes researchers choose to concentrate on medians rather than means. The primary reason is that the median often better reflects the central point in the data when the distribution is skewed. While we will not concentrate on this heavily in this text, there are a number of non-parametric statistical procedures which rely upon the median rather than the mean. If your variables have distributions which do not reasonably conform to the normal curve, one option is to explore non-parametric statistical procedures and rely heavily on medians as summary statistics of central tendency.

Exploring Distributions of Data

    A **distribution** refers to the spread of the data. Rather than looking for the central point in the data, the concern in examining a distribution is to get a sense of the way in which the data are dispersed. One of the most useful statistical depictions of distributions is the **stem and leaf** plot, which you should have by now observed emerges near the bottom of the *Explore* output. If a stem and leaf plot is not displayed when you run *Explore*, examine whether *Display Both* is selected in the *Explore* window.

    The stem and leaf plot, incidentally, was developed as a quick and dirty way of examining a distribution by using pencil and paper. Stem and leaf plots work like histograms (see Chapter 5) to show the distribution of data in a pictorial manner. To illustrate how a stem and leaf plot is constructed, examine the sorted output of the variable CRC348 (Rape Rate 1995) in Table 3.1 and the stem and leaf plot in Table 3.2.

Table 3.1 Rapes per 100,000 Population

STATE	RAPE RATE	STATE	RAPE RATE
NEBRASKA	19	WYOMING	34
WEST VIRGINIA	21	GEORGIA	35
MAINE	21	ILLINOIS	36
IOWA	21	KANSAS	36
NORTH DAKOTA	22	ARKANSAS	37
WISCONSIN	23	MISSISSIPPI	39
CONNECTICUT	23	COLORADO	39
NEW YORK	23	SOUTH DAKOTA	41
NEW JERSEY	24	OREGON	41
PENNSYLVANIA	25	MARYLAND	42
MONTANA	25	LOUISIANA	42
RHODE ISLAND	27	UTAH	42
VIRGINIA	27	OHIO	43
VERMONT	28	OKLAHOMA	44
HAWAII	28	TEXAS	45
IDAHO	28	TENNESSEE	47
MASSACHUSETTS	29	SOUTH CAROLINA	47
NEW HAMPSHIRE	29	FLORIDA	48
ALABAMA	31	DISTRICT OF COLUMBIA	52
KENTUCKY	31	MINNESOTA	56
MISSOURI	32	NEW MEXICO	56
NORTH CAROLINA	32	WASHINGTON	59
INDIANA	33	NEVADA	61
CALIFORNIA	33	MICHIGAN	62
ARIZONA	33	DELAWARE	80
		ALASKA	80

Table 3.2 Rape Rate 1995 Stem-and-Leaf Plot

Frequency	Stem & Leaf
1.00	1. 9
17.00	2. 11123334557788899
14.00	3. 11223334566799
11.00	4. 11222345778
4.00	5. 2669
2.00	6. 12
2.00 Extremes	(>=80)

Stem width: 10.00
Each leaf: 1 case(s)

The stem and leaf plot is constructed by taking the sorted values of the data and incorporating them in a systematic manner to produce a pictorial depiction of data. As the name implies, the pictorial depiction is constructed of two parts: the stems and the leaves. The stems, located on the left of the stem and leaf plot, are determined by the initial digits in the value of each case. The leaves, are constructed by entering the following digit for each case. For example, on the above stem and leaf display, the first row represents Nebraska, which had a rape rate of 19. The stem for Nebraska is 1, the leaf is 9. Because no other state had a rape rate below 20, Nebraska is the only case represented in the first row. The second row represents each state which had a rape rate of 20-29. The stem groups these states, using the initial digit 2 (indicating "20 something"). Each state is represented in the leaf by registering the remaining digit and these digits are entered in numeric order. The longest series of leaves are associated with stems with the greatest frequencies of occurrence. The above stem and leaf plot reveals that most states have a rape rate somewhere between 20 and 50.

Table 3.3 illustrates the manual process of building a stem and leaf plot (this represents the second row of the above stem and leaf plot). West Virginia's stem is 2, its leaf is 1. Maine's stem is 2, its leaf is 1. Iowa's stem is 2, its leaf is 1. North Dakota's stem is 2, its leaf is 2. This continues on until the values of the leaves increase to the point where the stem turns to 3 (indicating "30 something").

Table 3.3 Constructing a Stem and Leaf Plot Manually

Stem	Leaf	
2	1	← West Virginia
2	11	← Maine
2	111	← Iowa
2	1112	← North Dakota
2	11123334557788899	← New Hampshire
3	1	← Alabama
3	11	← Kentucky
	Etc.	

If a few of the states have stem values extraordinarily low or high, they will be grouped as "extremes" at the top or bottom of the stem and leaf plot. In the case of the above stem and leaf plot, Delaware (80) and Alaska (80) are classified as extremes.

Box plots are another effective way of examining the dispersion of the data using graphic techniques (Figure 3.6).

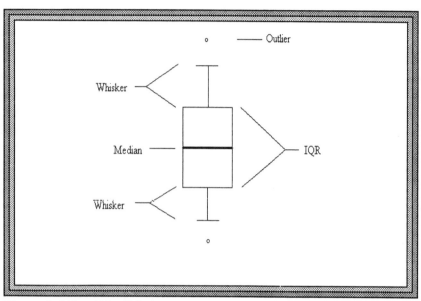

Figure 3.6 Box Plot Diagram

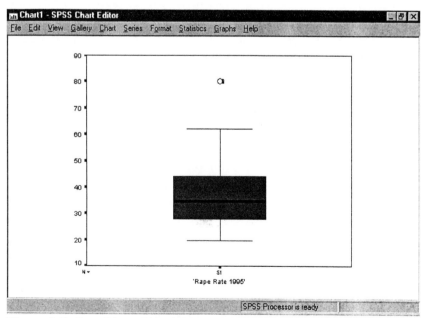

Figure 3.7 Box Plot of Variable CRC348

You can generate a box plot of data using the *Explore* command. If a box plot is not displayed when you run *Explore*, examine whether "*Display:* Both" is selected in the *Explore* window.

> *Statistics*
> > *Summarize*
> > > *Explore*
> > > > *Display:* Both

The box plot operates on non-parametric principles. Rather than concentrating on the mean, it concentrates on displaying the data in reference to the median. The median is represented by the line inside of the main box. Remember that 50% of the cases fall above and 50% of the cases fall below this line and in the case of CRC348 the median is 34.4. The main box (dark shaded) represents the interquartile range (IQR) and captures the middle 50% of the cases. Note in the above box plot (Figure 3.7) that the IQR begins at 27 and ends at 44. From this box plot, we know that 50% of the cases fall between 27 and 44. The IQR for this box plot is 17 (44-27=17). The "whiskers" (the thin lines extending out from the main box) are 1.5 IQRs from the median. The whiskers extend to the last case which falls within this distance from the main box. Those cases which are outside the whiskers are termed "outliers" and are signified by small circles. The number next to the outlier refers to the state number.

Box plots are handy because they yield very poignant depictions of the distribution of the data. For instance, from a box plot, we learn whether the data are concentrated at higher or lower values by examining the location of the median in relationship to the box and the whiskers. One other advantage of box plots is that they also quickly reveal whether a select few outlying cases are likely to influence our summary descriptions of data. You will see in the next chapter that outliers can have a profound effect on influencing our interpretations of how one variable affects another variable. In the case of rape rates, the box plot reveals that 2 outlying states are atypically placed in relation to the distribution of the rest of the states.

The *Explore* command also gives a number of other (non-pictorial) indicators of dispersion. Frankly, I rely more on visual depictions of dispersion than on numerical indicators when I'm analyzing data. Procedures such as stem and leaf plots and box plots provide more information than a single statistic. However, while statistics arguably give less information, they are often effectively used in tables to give readers a good indication of how great the data are dispersed away from the mean.

The **standard deviation** is a statistic used to measure the spread of data. It is constructed to estimate the degree to which we can expect proportions of the cases in a variable to fall within a specified range about the mean. The greater the dispersion of the data away from the mean results in higher standard deviations. Conversely, the tighter the concentration of data around the mean the smaller the standard deviation will be.

If the researcher knows the mean and the standard deviation, s/he has a good indication of whether any case is typical or atypical of the vast majority of cases. Plus or minus one standard deviation from the mean captures 68% of the cases of a variable. Plus or minus two standard deviations from the mean captures about 95% of the cases of a variable. Plus or minus three standard deviations from the mean captures about 99% of the cases of a variable. Thus a small standard deviation indicates that the data are not very dispersed and a large standard deviation indicates that the data are widely dispersed.

As point of illustration, return to variable CRC348 (Rape Rate 1995). Using the *Explore* command, you find that this variable has a standard deviation of 14.1 and a mean of 37.8. If plus or minus one standard deviation from the mean captures 68% of the cases, we know that 68% of the cases of variable CRC348 fall within the range 23.7-51.9. How did I arrive at this?

Mean - St.Dev=Low Value	Mean + St.Dev = High Value
37.8 - 14.1 = 23.7	37.8 + 14.1 = 51.9

Suppose we don't know anything about our data except for the standard deviation and the mean and somebody starts talking about Nevada when they discuss the incidence of rape. We know that Nevada has a rape rate of 61/100,000. We know by looking at the standard deviation in relationship to the mean, that over 68% of the cases fall closer to the mean than Nevada. If we are to discuss the incidence of rape, Nevada should be considered as having a relatively high rape problem in comparison to other states. We also know, by looking at the standard deviation in relation to the mean, that there is considerable variation in rape rates from state to state.

Computing New Variables

One of the strengths of using computers to do statistical analysis is the ease with which data can be reconfigured to suit the researcher's needs. Because the data come to us in one form, it does not mean that the data must continue to adhere to that form forever. In some circumstances we may want to generate a new variable which uses data from two or more existing variables.

For instance, it is not surprising that California had a larger *number* of rapes in 1995 than Oklahoma. (You can check this by examining variable CRC345 (Rapes 1995). In 1995, California had 10,554 rapes reported and Oklahoma had only 1,461 rapes. The data, while informative, are not especially meaningful from a research perspective because population sizes of both states are so different. How then, are we to compare rape in California with Oklahoma if both states have such different populations? The answer is to combine the incidence of rape with population in such a way that we are able to obtain a rape rate. A **rate** is a ratio of two variables which indicates the number of actual occurrences in reference to the potential number of occurrences. A rape rate allows us to estimate how many rapes occur against every 100,000 people. Because the population base of the statistic is now made constant, California and Oklahoma become comparable. If we sort the data according to variable CRC348, we learn that in relationship to its population base California actually has a lower frequency of rape (33/100,000) than does Oklahoma (44/100,000).

Rates, however, are not always provided in available data sets. In such circumstances it is necessary to generate new variables and create rates. Suppose, for instance, that a law enforcement agency asks you to determine where the police department should be focusing efforts to control violent crime. Agencies such as this have limited funds which they must use to fight murders, bombings, rapes, and other violent crimes. One solution would be to calculate the degree to which each of these types of violent acts contributes to the overall number of violent crimes. This would involve computing a new variable.

The *Compute* command involves using existing variables to calculate the values for a new variable. SPSS enables us to calculate a new variable by using the *compute* command from the *transform* menu:

> *Transform*
>> *Compute.*

In order to calculate the percentage of violent crimes which are rapes involves combining information from variables CRC316 (Violent Crimes 1995) with CRC345 (Rapes 1995). Use the *Compute* command to calculate a new *target* variable "RAPEPCT." You can also *label* the new variable "Rapes as % of Violent Crimes 1995" from the *Compute* window.

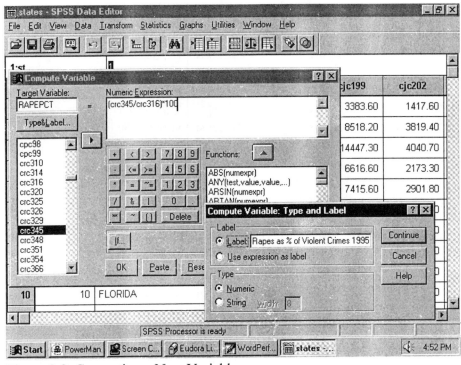

Figure 3.8 Computing a New Variable

Figure 3.8 shows how *compute* commands generates a the new *target* variable name "RAPEPCT" using the following formula:

(CRC345 /CRC316)*100
(Rapes 1995/Violent Crimes 1995) multiplied by 100

Case Summaries [a]

	RAPEPCT Rapes as % of Violent Crimes 1995	STATE
1	5.02	ALABAMA
2	10.42	ALASKA
3	4.71	ARIZONA
4	6.73	ARKANSAS
5	3.46	CALIFORNIA
6	8.97	COLORADO
7	5.84	CONNECTICUT
8	11.06	DELAWARE
9	1.98	DISTRICT OF COLUMBIA
10	4.54	FLORIDA
11	5.37	GEORGIA
12	9.58	HAWAII
13	8.81	IDAHO
14	3.66	ILLINOIS
15	6.34	INDIANA
16	6.15	IOWA
17	8.69	KANSAS
18	8.74	KENTUCKY
19	4.24	LOUISIANA
20	16.25	MAINE
21	4.28	MARYLAND
22	4.21	MASSACHUSETTS
23	9.01	MICHIGAN
24	15.80	MINNESOTA
25	7.77	MISSISSIPPI
26	4.84	MISSOURI
27	15.16	MONTANA
28	5.07	NEBRASKA
29	6.48	NEVADA
30	25.34	NEW HAMPSHIRE
31	4.04	NEW JERSEY
32	6.91	NEW MEXICO
33	2.81	NEW YORK
34	4.99	NORTH CAROLINA
35	26.26	NORTH DAKOTA
36	8.99	OHIO
37	6.71	OKLAHOMA
38	7.98	OREGON
39	5.90	PENNSYLVANIA
40	7.33	RHODE ISLAND
41	4.82	SOUTH CAROLINA
42	19.76	SOUTH DAKOTA
43	6.11	TENNESSEE
44	6.89	TEXAS
45	13.00	UTAH
46	23.84	VERMONT
47	7.52	VIRGINIA
48	12.22	WASHINGTON
49	10.10	WEST VIRGINIA
50	8.29	WISCONSIN
51	13.52	WYOMING
Total N	51	51

a. Limited to first 100 cases.

Figure 3.9 Case Summaries as a Check for Accuracy

It is extremely important that each time a compute procedure is performed that the new data be analyzed to confirm that they are accurately calculated. One way to do this is to list the new rate with data that can be checked for its accuracy. For example, I know that no percentage could possibly be higher than 100%, and I would also be surprised if any state reported rapes as the major type of violent crime. The data can be checked by using the command:

> *Statistics*
> > *Summarize*
> > > *Case Summaries*
> > > > *Variables:* RAPEPCT
> > > > STATE.

Using the *Case Summaries* output, you can examine the percentages to see if the calculations seem accurate (Figure 3.9). You may find it interesting to perform a *Sort* on RAPEPCT to examine which states have the highest proportion of rapes to violent crime. Where does your state rank? In the District of Columbia, rapes constitute only 2% of the violent crimes, but in New Hampshire they constitute 25% of the violent crimes. If you were a consultant to each of these states, would you offer the same advice on where to channel resources to fight violent crime?

Recoding Existing Variables

There are many circumstances where a researcher may want to **recode** (or reconfigure) the data in an existing variable. In some circumstances, the researcher may be doing this to make the data conform to the existing conceptualization of a particular issue. For example, alcohol consumption is often measured as a continuous variable (0,1,2,3,4...drinks/day). However, American culture emphasizes the distinction between abstainers, social drinkers, and alcoholics. To bring the data in line with the conceptualization requires recoding the continuous variable into the form of an categorical variable, distinguishing "nonusers" (0 drinks/day) from "moderate users" (1-2 drinks/day) from "heavy users" (3 or more drinks/day).

One word of forewarning, before we begin recoding variables: **when variables are recoded their form changes forever**. If a researcher recodes his/her data and then saves the data replacing the old data set, the transformation becomes permanent and there is no way to backtrack and recover nuances in the data which were inevitably lost during the recode procedures. Also, if there is an error in the recoding commands, and if the data are saved and replaced, that error will forever be in the data set. There is an easy way to protect a data set from this danger within the *recode* command procedures by always recoding a variable into a different variable.

> *Transform*
> > *Recode*
> > > *Into Different Variables*

By selecting "*Into Different Variables,*" the *recode* procedure automatically creates a new variable, recoded from the old variable. If you select "*Into Same Variables,*" SPSS will replace the values in that existing variable and irrevocably alter your data.

   To illustrate the recoding procedure, let's suppose that we want to distinguish those states which performed an execution from 1977-1995 from those states which have not performed any executions. We already have a continuous variable, CPC77 (Prisoners Executed: 1977-95), and desire to recode it into a dichotomous variable. Using the *Recode* command, in the first window select variable CPC77 and identify the new *Output Variable* as RECODE1. *Label* the output variable as "Dichotomy Recode of Executions." You should duplicate Figure 3.10 and Figure 3.11 in recoding this variable.

   To begin the recode procedure, select *Old and New Values* to reveal another window. You will be recoding the old values in CPC77 so that states with no executions are coded as 0 and states with executions are coded as 1 in variable RECODE 1. Note that you can replace values one at a time, or select a range of old values to be recoded as a single value.

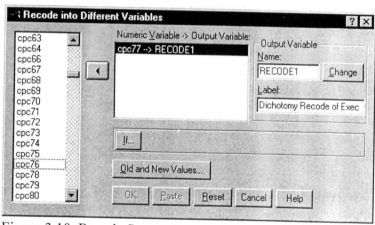

Figure 3.10 Recode Screen 1

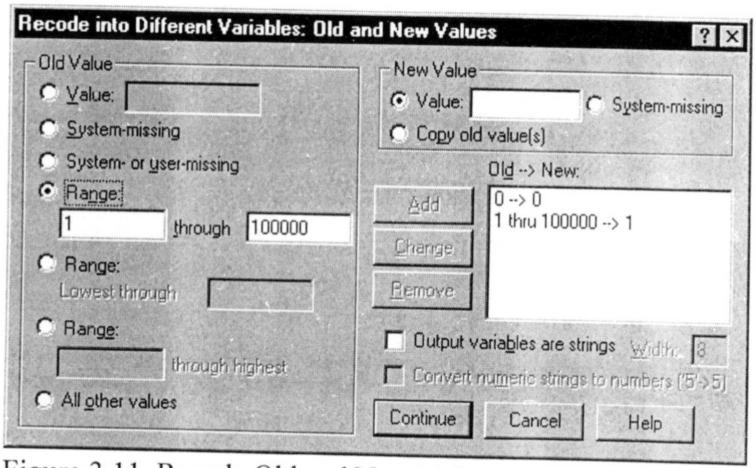

Figure 3.11 Recode Old and New Values

After recoding the variable, to make sure that the new variable is recoded accurately use:

> *Statistics*
> > *Summarize*
> > > *Case Summaries*
> > > > *Variables:* CPC77
> > > > > RECODE1

Using the *Frequencies* command, determine the percent of states which performed an execution from 1977-1995 by analyzing variable RECODE1. You should find that 51% of the states performed at least one execution from 1977-1995.

Summary

In this chapter you have learned some of the essential skills associated with univariate analysis. To recapitulate:

Univariate analysis involves understanding the characteristics of a single variable in isolation from other variables.

The mean, median, and mode are measures of central tendency, and can be found using the *Explore*, *Descriptives,* and *Frequencies* commands.

Dispersion is commonly measured with standard deviations, stem and leaf plots, and box plots. These can be found using the *Explore* commands.

New variables can be created from old variables using the *Compute* command. This is useful for generating rates or indices.

Recoding variables involves changing the values in one variable to enable appropriate use of advanced statistical procedures and to mold data to fit existing conceptualizations.

Key Terms

Univariate Analysis	Sorting Data	Measures of Central Tendency
Mean	Median	Mode
Distributions	Stem and Leaf Plot	Box Plot
Standard Deviation	Computing Variables	Recoding Variables

References and Further Reading

Gilbert, Dennis and Joseph Kahl. 1993. *The New American Class Structure*. Belmont CA: Wadsworth.

Hamilton, Lawrence. 1990. *Modern Data Analysis: A First Course in Applied Statistics*. Brooks/Cole Publishing: Pacific Grove California.

Levin, Jack and James Fox. 1997. *Elementary Statistics in Social Research*. Longman: New York.

Chapter 3 Exercises

Name_____   Date_____

1. Using the *Sort* command and *Case Summaries*, determine the states which score the highest and lowest levels of incidence of the following variables:

    A. CJC205 (Juvenile Arrest Rate: Violent Crime 1995)

              _____   _____

                         Lowest State   Highest State

    B. CRC508 (Rate of Reported Hate Crimes 1995)

              _____   _____

                         Lowest State   Highest State

    C. DMS492 (Divorce Rate 1995)

              _____   _____

                         Lowest State   Highest State

    D. HTS384 (Death Rate by AIDS 1994)

              _____   _____

                         Lowest State   Highest State

2. Using *Explore,* determine the mean and median for the following variables. Examine the stem and leaf displays and determine which is more appropriate to use as the measure of central tendency.

    A. CJC205 (Juvenile Arrest Rate: Violent Crime 1995)

           _____   _____

                 Mean   Median

      Circle the measure would you use as the measure of central tendency: Mean   Median
         Why did you make this selection?

    B. CRC508 (Rate of Reported Hate Crimes 1995)

           _____   _____

                 Mean   Median

      Circle the measure would you use as the measure of central tendency: Mean   Median
         Why did you make this selection?

C. DMS492 (Divorce Rate 1995)

_____   _____
          Mean   Median

Circle the measure would you use as the measure of central tendency: Mean   Median
Why did you make this selection?

D. HTS384 (Death Rate by AIDS 1994)

_____   _____
          Mean   Median

Circle the measure would you use as the measure of central tendency: Mean   Median
Why did you make this selection?

3. Generate a new variable MURDPCT and label it "Murders as % of Violent Crimes" using *Compute*. Use the following formula to generate the new variable.

(CRC326 / CRC316)*100
(Murders 1995 divided by Violent Crimes 1995) multiplied by 100

What is the mean of this new variable?   _____

Which state has the highest percentage of violent crimes which are murders?

_____

Which state has the lowest percentage of violent crimes which are murders?

_____

4. *Compute* a new variable VCPCT which determines the percentage of crimes which are violent crimes. Use variables CRC310 (Crimes 1995) and CRC316 (Violent Crimes 1995) to compute the new variable.

Which state has the highest percentage of crimes which are violent crimes?

_____

Which state has the lowest percentage of crimes which are violent crimes?

_____

What percentage of crimes are violent crimes in your state?

_____

What is the mean of VCPCT? _____

5. Using the variable REGION4, *Recode* the variable into a new variable SOUTH.   SOUTH will be used to indicate whether a state is located in the south or not. Recode states which are coded as "South" in REGION4 to equal 1. Recode all other regions to equal 0.

REGION4	SOUTH
1=NorthEast	0=NonSouth
2=MidWest	0=NonSouth
3=South	1=South
4=West	0=NonSouth

To recode these data use the procedure:
> *Transform*
>> *Recode*
>>> *Into Different Variables*

Print (and double check) the results using:
> *Statistics*
>> *Summarize*
>>> *Case Summaries*
>>>> (STATE REGION4 SOUTH)

Chapter 4
Bivariate Analysis

Overview

Bivariate analysis involves examining relationships between two variables. Unlike univariate analysis, which examines the characteristics of individual variables, bivariate analysis examines the ways in which the characteristics of one variable are associated with the characteristics of another variable. Some examples of questions open to bivariate analysis include:

Is educational attainment associated with race?

Is drug use associated with income?

Does religious affiliation vary by geographic location?

Is crime associated with concentrated poverty?

All of these questions involve comparing two variables to see if there is an association or co-relationship of one variable with the other. In this chapter you will learn how to determine the extent to which two variables are associated with one another. This includes determining statistical significance, as well as the procedures involved in constructing cross tabulations, comparisons of means, and correlations.

Statistical Significance

Statistical significance is a term which is used to assess the degree to which a researcher can rule out chance as the explanation for any relationship found. When a researcher determines that a relationship is a statistically significant relationship, it does not mean that the relationship is important, only that random chance or random co-variation in the variables is an unlikely explanation for the relationship being discussed.

There are a number of methods of calculating statistical significance and we will not concern ourselves with the formulas involved in these calculations. We will be concerned with the interpretation of the statistics used to understand statistical significance. You will see that the significance statistics vary depending on the type of analysis being performed, but the method of interpreting these statistics is similar.

Statistical significance is calculated by analyzing two things: the strength of the association and the sample size. Before discussing the interpretation of significance tests, it is important to understand how magnitudes of effect and sample sizes influence the "significance" of a relationship observed between two variables. Suppose Springfield has a nuclear power plant and the residents of Springfield are concerned that the power plant might be affecting their community's infant mortality rate. The residents ask a researcher to perform a study to determine if the nuclear power plant is causing the infant mortality rate to increase. The researcher understands that infant mortality rates fluctuate on an annual basis in every community. Some years mortality rates are low, some years they are high, and it seems that random chance plays a role in these fluctuations. This is akin to us expecting a coin tossed ten times to yield five heads and five tails, but it is not unusual to have a moderate variation from this expectation in any given ten coin tosses. The researcher needs to rule out the role random chance plays before she can conclude that the plant does or does not influence infant mortality rates.

One methodology would be to compare Springfield's mortality rates over time. If the researcher only has two years of observation, one pre-power plant and one post-power plant, it is very likely that the two rates will differ to some extent simply due to chance. However, if the difference in the rates is huge, she would be able to have greater confidence that the findings are statistically significant and not just an artifact of random fluctuation.

This study can be strengthened considerably by obtaining a large sample of years. The researcher could collect 20 years of data prior to the power plant operating and 20 years of data after the power plant began operations. With the increased sample size, magnitudes of effects can actually be smaller and still be statistically significant. With a large enough sample size, very small effects can be interpreted as statistically meaningful.

The formulas for statistical significance take into account both the magnitude of effect and sample size. From these calculations, a probability score is generated which indicates the likelihood that the results achieved are due to the influence of random chance. The higher the probability score, the greater the likelihood that random chance produced the fluctuation. The lower the probability score, the greater the confidence that there is an actual association between the two variables being studied.

Probability scores can vary from .00 to 1.00. A score of 1.00 indicates that there is a 100% probability that random chance alone could have produced these findings and that we should place no confidence in any fluctuation in the numbers as being statistically meaningful. If the probability score is .50, this indicates there is a 50% probability that the findings could have been produced simply by the influence of random chance. If the score is .10, only ten times out of every hundred times we would find magnitudes of effect this large due to the influence of chance. If the score was .01, there is only one chance in a hundred that the relationship between the variables could be attributed to the influence of random chance. While I have phrased each of these interpretations of probability scores in different ways, the point is the same: the lower the probability score, the greater the confidence that the relationship is statistically meaningful.

At what level does a probability score become statistically significant? This is actually a complicated issue, because it depends on the type of question being asked and the types of effects a researcher is looking at. Suppose that our hypothetical power plant study had shown an increase in infant mortality with a significance level of .30. This means that there is only a 30% chance that the findings are due to the influence of random chance. Acting as a parent (and not as a social scientist), if I were contemplating living in the community, I would probably take the findings very seriously.

Norms of social research advocate a more conservative standard in asserting statistical significance. Usually relationships are only seriously considered if there is only a small chance of the results being due to chance. If the sample size is small, then a probability score of .10 or lower ($p < .10$) is generally accepted as statistically significant in social science research. If the sample size is moderate to large, probability scores of $p < .05$ and $p < .01$ are considered to be statistically significant. This means that there is only a 5% or 1% chance that the results of the study are due to the influence of chance. If the nuclear power plant study had only achieved probability scores of $p < .30$, most social science researchers would conclude that the data do not indicate that a relationship exists or that further study is needed before the relationship can be determined as existing.

It is important to note that people sometimes misinterpret the statistical significance score as indicating that there is a strong relationship. With a large enough sample size, very weak relationships can be revealed to be statistically significant. Statistical significance tells us nothing about the relationship other than informing us of the likelihood that chance is the explanation for the findings. Relating this back to the hypothetical nuclear power plant study, suppose we find a statistically significant relationship ($p < .05$). It is still possible that the relationship is very weak. It is also possible that the data could indicate that a power plant could *lower* the infant mortality rate. The statistical significance score does not address these other possibilities, only the possibility that random chance is a likely explanation for the findings.

Analyzing Bivariate Relationships

Statistics are part of our toolkit as social science researchers. The concern with data analysis is finding the right statistic for the job. There are three dominant procedures for measuring bivariate relationships: cross tabulations, comparing means, and correlations. Each procedure is designed to deal with different types of data. In order to correctly perform a bivariate analysis, it is necessary to understand the structure of each variable (recall this is done through univariate analysis). **Categorical variables** are structured into discrete groupings, such as male/female, North/East/West/South, employed/unemployed, White/Black/Hispanic, etc. Bivariate relationships between two categorical variables are analyzed through cross tabulations. **Continuous variables** are structured to reveal continuity of measures, such as temperature in degrees, population in numbers, or incidence of mortality. Bivariate relationships between two continuous variables are analyzed through correlations. Comparisons of means are designed to analyze relationships between categorical and continuous variables. Table 4.1 shows how each of these statistical procedures requires different types of data.

Table 4.1   Bivariate Statistical Procedures, Variable Expectations, and Significance Tests

Statistical Procedure	Types of Variables	Significance Tests
Crosstabs	2 categorical	Chi-Square, Phi, Cramer's V
Compare Means	1 categorical; 1 continuous	ANOVA
Correlations	2 continuous	t tests

Cross Tabulations

Crosstabs is a truncation of the phrase "cross tabulation." A cross tabulation is produced by constructing a grid of all possible intersections between two categorical variables. When the cells of this grid are filled according to the occurrence of intersecting values, associations between two variables become apparent. Assuming that the cases in the data are evenly divided, if there are comparable numbers of cases in each cell between groups, then there is no relationship between the two variables. However, if the cases are disproportionately located in the cells between groups, then there is likely a statistical relationship.

Normally samples are not equally divided. For example, surveys tend to over-sample women and under-sample men. Religious groups are not equally divided (e.g., there are more Protestants than Jews in the United States). For this reason, cross tabulations are usually constructed to compare percentages rather than numerical frequencies.

To illustrate how to construct and interpret a cross tabulation, lets compare people's attitudes concerning suicide using the GSS96.SAV data set. Open the data set and use the following commands to generate the windows (Figures 4.1, 4.2, 4.3) and output (Figures 4.4, 4.5, 4.6) displayed below:

> *Statistics*
>> *Summarize*
>>> *Crosstabs*
>>>> *Rows*:   SUICIDE1
>>>> *Columns*: SEX
>>>>> *Statistics*:   Chi-square
>>>>>   Phi and Cramer's V
>>>>> *Cells*:   Observed
>>>>>   Percentages Column.

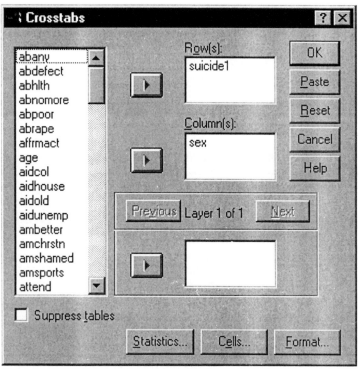

Figure 4.1 Crosstabs Dialogue Box

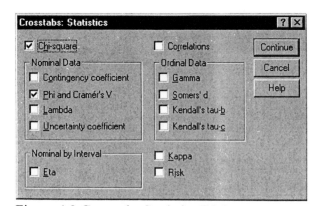

Figure 4.2 Crosstabs Statistics Dialogue Box

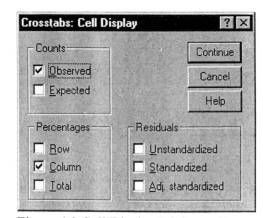

Figure 4.3 Cell Display Dialogue Box

As standard practice, I find it easiest to consistently put the dependent variable as the row variable and the independent variable as the column variable. In this case, because I believe gender may influence attitudes toward suicide, sex is the column variable and suicide is the row variable. The advantage of this system is that it provides a consistent approach to interpreting cross tabulations.

Because I want to compare groups of people by their sex, I use the column percentages to interpret the findings. The column percentages divide the sample into subsamples based on sex. Conceptually, you can think of this as segregating the group according to their sex and then polling them on the suicide question. So long as the dependent variable is the row variable, generating the column percentages will usually be the correct method of constructing the cross tabulation.

SUICIDE1 SUICIDE IF INCURABLE DISEASE * SEX RESPONDENTS SEX Crosstabulation

| | | | SEX RESPONDENTS SEX | | |
			MALE	FEMALE	Total
SUICIDE1 SUICIDE IF INCURABLE DISEASE	YES	Count	566	631	1197
		% within SEX RESPONDENTS SEX	66.0%	57.5%	61.2%
	NO	Count	248	414	662
		% within SEX RESPONDENTS SEX	28.9%	37.7%	33.8%
	DK	Count	44	53	97
		% within SEX RESPONDENTS SEX	5.1%	4.8%	5.0%
Total		Count	858	1098	1956
		% within SEX RESPONDENTS SEX	100.0%	100.0%	100.0%

Figure 4.4 Cross Tabulation Output

Chi-Square Tests

	Value	df	Asymp. Sig. (2-tailed)
Pearson Chi-Square	16.795[a]	2	.000
Likelihood Ratio	16.918	2	.000
Linear-by-Linear Association	.938	1	.333
N of Valid Cases	1956		

a. 0 cells (.0%) have expected count less than 5. The minimum expected count is 42.55.

Figure 4.5 Chi Square Output

Symmetric Measures

		Value	Approx. Sig.
Nominal by Nominal	Phi	.093	.000
	Cramer's V	.093	.000
N of Valid Cases		1956	

Figure 4.6 Phi and Cramer's V Significance Tests

By examining the crosstab table in Figure 4.4, it seems apparent that there is a relationship between sex and acceptance of suicide. Men are more willing than women to say that they believe it is acceptable for people to commit suicide if they have an incurable disease. This finding is produced by comparing percentages within the cross tabulation (66% of men versus 57% of women saying "yes"). The count (located at the top of each cell) provides supplemental information on how many cases fall within each cell. Researchers should be careful of overestimating the importance of percentages produced through "thin cells" (cells with very few cases represented). This is a problem which largely emerges in small samples, but is not likely to pose a major problem in data sets as large as the GSS.

Figures 4.5 and 4.6 show the results of the significance tests. SPSS offers a number of different significance tests, but it is beyond the purposes of this text to detail the relative strengths and weaknesses of each test. I have chosen in this case to run three of the most widely accepted significance tests, Chi-square, Phi, and Cramer's V. Each of these tests reveals that the relationship is statistically significant because the probability scores are revealed to be less than .05. These probability scores are located in the columns labeled "Asymp. Sig." and "Approx. Sig." All of these tests reveal a probability score of .000. There is less than a 1/1000 chance that the relationship observed between sex and attitudes toward suicide are due to the influence of random chance.

Comparison of Means

Comparisons of means tests are used to assess the relationship between a continuous variable with a categorical variable. For instance, age may influence attitudes towards suicide, but because age is a continuous variable it is not immediately conducive to the cross tabulation procedure. If we did try a cross tabulation of these variables using GSS data, we are likely to have each year of a person's adult life represented in a cross tabulation. You can try this and I think you will see that the cross tabulation will be so large, and some cells so thin, that analysis of the data will not be easy. One solution would be to group people by age (e.g., age 18-25, 26-35, etc.) and then perform the crosstab. A more elegant solution would be to compare the mean ages of people who believe in the right to suicide with the mean ages of those who do not. In SPSS, this is performed through the *Compare Means* command.

In the *Compare Means* procedure, SPSS assumes that the dependent variable will be the continuous variable. In this case, however, age is the continuous variable and attitude about suicide is the independent variable. For this procedure we are going to pretend that age is the dependent variable and attitude about suicide is the independent variable for the statistical procedure (Figure 4.7). This will do no harm and we can shift our analysis of the statistics in accordance with the hypothesis that age affects attitude toward suicide. The comparison of means uses ANOVA (analysis of variance) as the significance test. To test the relationship of age and suicide attitude, the output reproduced here can be made using the following commands:

Statistics
　　Compare Means
　　　　Means
　　　　　　Dependent List: AGE
　　　　　　Independent List: SUICIDE1
　　　　　　　　Options: Anova table and eta.

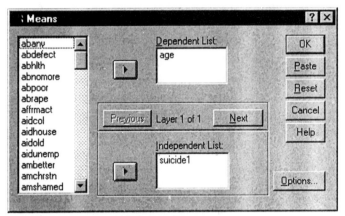

Figure 4.7 Means Dialogue Box

Report

AGE AGE OF RESPONDENT

YES	Mean	43.51
	N	1194
	Std. Deviation	16.14
NO	Mean	46.68
	N	662
	Std. Deviation	17.66
DK	Mean	49.31
	N	96
	Std. Deviation	19.05
Total	Mean	44.87
	N	1952
	Std. Deviation	16.91

Figure 4.8 Report Table

ANOVA Table

			Sum of Squares	df	Mean Square	F	Sig.
AGE AGE OF RESPONDENT * SUICIDE1 SUICIDE IF INCURABL DISEASE	Between Groups	(Combined)	6290.135	2	3145.067	11.112	.000
	Within Groups		551618	1949	283.026		
	Total		557908	1951			

Figure 4.9 ANOVA Table

In the output from the *Compare Means*, we will concentrate on the Report (Figure 4.8) and the ANOVA table (Figure 4.9). The Report table compares the average age (mean) of advocates with the average age of people opposed to the suicide rights for people with incurable diseases. The Report indicates the average age of people who advocate suicide rights is 43.5 years, the average age for people against is 46.6 years, and for those who "don't know" (DK), the average age is 49.3 years. There appears to be a three-year average age difference between each group. Examining the ANOVA table, we find the significance test (Sig.) registers a probability of .000. This is a statistically significant relationship.

Correlations

Correlations are designed to measure the strength of the relationship between two continuous variables. Generally, when social scientists discuss a correlation they are referring to the Pearson's correlation coefficient. This coefficient provides a succinct description of the degree to which two continuous variables are related to one another. The Pearson's correlation coefficient (from here on the "correlation") always varies somewhere between -1 and +1. The closer the correlation is to either +1 or -1, the stronger the relationship between the two variables. Conversely, the closer the correlation is to 0, the weaker the correlation. A correlation of 0 indicates that there is absolutely no association between the two variables. Correlations of -1 and +1 indicate that there is a perfect linear association between the two variables.

The negative and positive signs indicate the direction of the relationships. A negative correlation indicates relationships in which increases in one variable are associated with decreases in the other variable. For example, research has shown a negative correlation between education and prejudice in that the more educated a person becomes, the less often s/he expresses prejudicial thoughts. A positive correlation, on the other hand, indicates a relationship in which increases in one variable are associated with increases in the other variable. For example, there is a positive correlation between education and income, in that the more educated a person becomes, the more likely s/he will earn a higher salary.

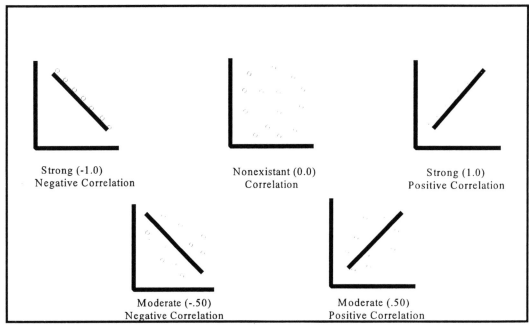

Figure 4.10 Graphic Depiction of Correlations

Let us return to the study of suicide using correlations. In a classic piece of research, the sociologist Emile Durkheim (1897) suggested that suicides are not only influenced by people's attitudes toward the act of suicide, but also by social forces which surround them. He suggested that places with high levels of social pathology (e.g., crime, divorce, substance abuse) will also have high levels of suicide. The reason is that suicide tends to be high in places with high levels of social disorganization.

We can test Durkheim's thesis using the STATES data set. Open this data and then run a correlation on the relationship between suicide and the divorce rate (Figures 4.11 and 4.12). If Durkheim is correct, we should expect to find a positive correlation between these two variables.

Statistics
> *Correlate*
>> *Bivariate*: HTS381 (Death Rate by Suicide 1994)
>>> DMS492 (Divorce Rate 1995)
>> *Pearson.*

Correlations

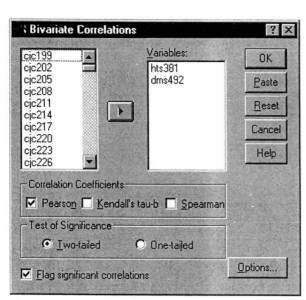

Figure 4.11 Correlation Dialogue Box

		HTS381 'Death Rate by Suicide 1994'	DMS492 'Divorce Rate 1995'
Pearson Correlation	HTS381 'Death Rate by Suicide 1994'	1.000	.752**
	DMS492 'Divorce Rate 1995'	.752**	1.000
Sig. (2-tailed)	HTS381 'Death Rate by Suicide 1994'		.000
	DMS492 'Divorce Rate 1995'	.000	
N	HTS381 'Death Rate by Suicide 1994'	51	47
	DMS492 'Divorce Rate 1995'	47	47

** Correlation is significant at the 0.01 level (2-tailed).

Figure 4.12 Correlation Output

The correlation between divorce and suicide offers strong support of Durkheim's thesis. There is a .752 correlation between these two variables. This relationship is statistically significant as well. This can be seen in two ways from the Correlations table. The 2-tailed significance test shows a probability of .000, indicating statistical significance. Also, correlation tables flag out significance with asterisks (**) next to the coefficients.

Summary

Bivariate relationships examine how characteristics of one variable are associated with characteristics of another variable. This chapter has concentrated on how to establish the existence of the statistical association using SPSS. There are three main ways of doing this, through crosstabs, comparisons of means, and correlations. For each method of determining a statistical association, there are accompanying significance tests. The significance tests inform the researcher if the association between the two variables is strong enough so that chance can be ruled out as a likely explanation for the observed relationship. It is up to the researcher to determine the direction of the relationship and the strength of the relationship by analyzing the output produced.

Key Terms

significance tests	categorical variables	continuous variables
correlations	comparisons of means	ANOVA
cross tabulations		

References and Further Reading

Hamilton, Lawrence. 1990. *Modern Data Analysis: A First Course in Applied Statistics*. Brooks/Cole Publishing: Pacific Grove California.

Levin, Jack and James Fox. 1997. *Elementary Statistics in Social Research*. Longman: New York.

Chapter 4 Exercises

Name_____   Date_____

1. A researcher examines a relationship between "sensitivity" and "cultural acceptance." As a result of her study she finds a correlation of .20 between these variables and a probability score of .25. On the basis of this study, can she conclude that sensitivity is associated with cultural acceptance? Explain.

2. A police force has increased its employment from five full-time officers in 1998 to eight full-time officers in 1999 in an effort to deter crime. They call you in to analyze whether their program has been effective and give you the following output to analyze. How would you interpret this cross tabulation to the police department?

| | Number of Arrests | |
	1998	1999
Property Crime Arrests	325	375
Violent Crime Arrests	120	119

$p < .03$

3. Using the GSS96 data, examine the relationship between attitudes toward abortion (ABANY "Abortion if Woman Wants for Any Reason") and the sex (SEX) of the respondent. Fill in the following information:

Percentage of men stating this is acceptable   _____

Percentage of women stating this is acceptable   _____

Probability score (chi square)   _____

Is the relationship statistically significant?   Yes   No

Can you explain this result?

4. Using the GSS96 data, examine the relationship between race (RACE) and whether a person used a condom during the last experience of intercourse (CONDOM).

Percentage of whites using condom   _____

Percentage of blacks using condom   _____

Probability score (chi square)   _____

Is the relationship statistically significant?   Yes   No

Can you explain this result?

5. Using the GSS96 data, examine the relationship between race (RACE) and the belief that whites are hurt by affirmative action (DISCAFF).

Percentage of whites saying "Likely" or "Very Likely"   _____

Percentage of blacks saying "Likely" or "Very Likely"   _____

Probability score (chi square)   _____

Is the relationship statistically significant?   Yes   No

Can you explain this result?

6. Astrologers assert that our birth dates influence our success (or lack thereof) in life. Test this assumption with the GSS96.SAV data by analyzing the relationship between ZODIAC (Respondent's Astrological Sign) with SEI (Respondent Socioeconomic Index). The SEI is an indicator of economic and social-economic attainment. The higher the SEI score, the more successful the respondent.

Mean SEI of Pisces   _____

Mean SEI of Taurus   _____

Mean SEI of your astrological sign   _____

Probability score (ANOVA)   _____

Is the relationship statistically significant?   Yes   No

On the basis of these data, would you say that astrologers are correct in their assertion of the power of the stars? Why?

7. Is there a relationship between a person's age (AGE) and the number of hours spent per day watching TV (TVHOURS)? Use the GSS96 data to test this relationship.

Correlation   _____

Probability (t test)   _____

Is the relationship statistically significant?   Yes   No

Who tends to watch the most TV?   Young Adults   Middle Age   Seniors

Can you explain this result?

8. Is there a relationship between the number of books in public libraries per capita (SCS155) and the high school dropout rate (SCS134)? Use the STATES data to examine this question. Summarize and interpret your findings below.

9. Is there a relationship between the average salary of classroom teachers (SCS130) and the public high school graduation rate (SCS133)? Use the STATES data to examine this question. Summarize and interpret your findings below.

10. Is there a relationship between the percent of the population which is black (DMS451) and the high school drop-out rate (SCS134)? Use the STATES data to examine this question.   Summarize and interpret your findings below.

Chapter 5
Graphing

Overview

    Computer programs such as SPSS have greatly contributed to our ability to analyze data using graphic images. Pictures of data, as opposed to numeric representations, are one of the most powerful ways to understand the complexities of social relationships. In this chapter we will revisit univariate and bivariate analysis, relying on graphical techniques to understand data. The first section of this chapter will analyze univariate graphing techniques, including pie charts, bar charts, histograms, and box plots. The second section of this chapter will introduce some bivariate graphing techniques, including bivariate box plots, bar graphs, and scatter plots. In this chapter you will learn the types of data suited to each graphic technique, as well as how to refine graphic presentation of data using SPSS.

Univariate Graphing

    Univariate graphing is a method of displaying distributions of individual variables. In this section we will also examine four common univariate graphing techniques: pie charts, bar graphs, histograms, and box plots. Pie charts and bar charts are designed to display the frequencies of categorical variables. Histograms and box plots are designed to display the distributions of continuous variables.

Table 5.1 Variable Formats and Univariate Graphing Procedures

Graphing Technique	Variable Format
Pie Charts	Categorical
Bar Charts	Categorical
Box Plots	Continuous
Histograms	Continuous

Pie Charts

The pie chart is one of the earliest popular methods of graphing distributions and is still used heavily in marketing and business to display pictorial descriptions of data. One reason for its popularity relates to the underlying conceptualization of the pie chart, which suggests that there is a limited amount of resources (the pie) which can be distributed in a variety of ways (the wedges). A pie chart quickly reveals if any resource is distributed equitably or inequitably, depending on the size of the wedges.

Pie charts require that the variable being represented be in the form of a categorical variable. Using the GSS96 data, we can construct a pie chart which displays the proportions of people expressing differing opinions concerning a woman's right to have an abortion "if she wants one for any reason" (ABANY) (Figure 5.1).

> *Graphs*
>> *Pie*
>>> *Data in Chart Are*: Summaries for groups of cases
>>> *Slices Represent*: $\underline{N}$ of cases (or % of cases)
>>> *Define Slices By*: ABANY
>>> *Titles*: Woman Can Have Abortion for Any Reason
>>>> (If missing values are incorporated into the pie chart, check *Options.*)

You will observe that the pie chart produced on your screen looks slightly different than that in your text. In order to format the pie chart to suit black and white print, I took advantage of some of the **Chart Editor** commands available in SPSS. You will inevitably want to explore these options, especially when it comes time to publish some of the graphic presentations you produce.

To access the *Chart Editor*, double click on the pie chart generated in the *Output Navigator* window (Figure 5.2). You should observe that the SPSS *Chart Editor* window opens as a consequence. To edit the chart, it is usually helpful to expand the *Chart Editor* window to fill the full screen using the icon in the upper right corner of the *Chart Editor* window.

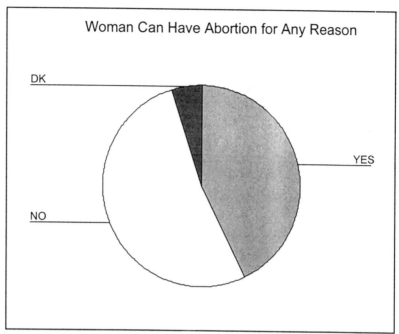

Figure 5.1 Pie Chart

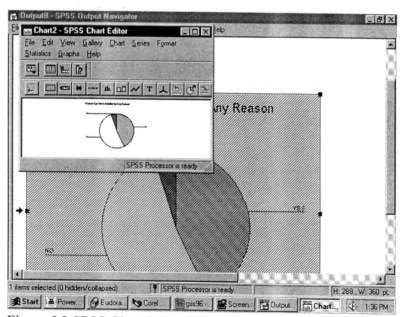

Figure 5.2 SPSS Chart Editor Window

In the case of the pie chart in Figure 5.1, I changed the colors of the wedges in the pie chart by using *Chart Editor* command:

> *Format*
> > *Color.*

I also moved the title to be justified on the left by using the command:

> *Format*
> > *Chart*
> > > *Title.*

Another option which is quite useful for pie charts is altering the fill pattern of the wedges. This can be accomplished by using the command:

> *Format*
> > *Fill Pattern.*

At this point you may want to take a few moments and explore the ways in which pie charts can be constructed and altered using a few different variables. Try to make charts which are informative, easy to interpret, and appropriately titled.

As mentioned above, pie charts are popular in business and marketing. They have largely fallen out of favor for social scientists because they are not always easy to interpret accurately. Discerning small (but sometimes very important) differences on the basis of wedge thickness can be difficult. For this reason, many researchers prefer using bar charts over pie charts.

Bar Charts

Bar charts are graphs which depict the frequencies of categorical variable values in terms of the height of individual bars. Each bar represents a different value in the variable. There are a variety of types of bar charts, including stacking bars on top of each other. We will explore some of the features by constructing a simple bar chart, which places value bars side-by-side in a single graph. To produce a bar chart of ABANY, perform the following commands:

> *Graphs*
> > *Bar*
> > > *Simple*
> > > > *Data in Chart Are*: Summaries for groups of cases
> > > > *Bars Represent*: % of cases
> > > > *Category Axis*: ABANY
> > > > *Titles*: Woman Can Have Abortion for Any Reason
> > > > (If missing values are incorporated into the graph, check *Options.*)

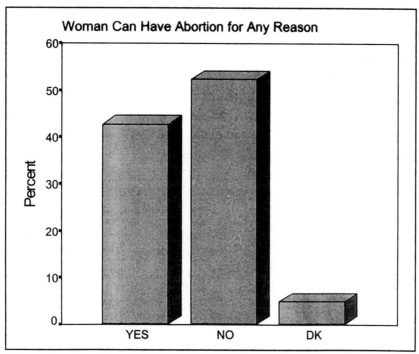

Figure 5.3 Bar Chart Output

Again, you will observe that your bar chart looks slightly different than the one represented in Figure 5.3. You can restructure your chart by using the *Chart Editor* window by double clicking on the graph generated in the *Output Navigator* window. Within the *Chart Editor* window, you can change the bar style to depict a three dimensional bar with the following commands:

> *Format*
> > *Bar Style*: 3-D effect.

You can change the color or shading on different segments of the bars with the command:

> *Format*
> > *Color.*

It is also useful in some circumstances to change the specifications for each axis. In the graph represented above, I made the following modifications:

Chart
> *Axis*
>> *Scale*
>>> *Title Justification*: Center
>> *Category*
>>> *Axis Title*: Opinion
>>> *Title Justification*: Center.

Now that you are familiar with the Chart Editor, you may find it useful to explore some of the other options available and customize some of your own bar charts.

Histograms

Histograms are designed to display continuous variables in graphic form. We have already discussed bell curves, which are also sometimes called normal curves or normal histograms. You can think of histograms working much like bar charts, displaying frequency of occurrence by the height of the point representing a particular value. The difference is that histograms are usually used to display the distributions of continuous variables. To accomplish this, histograms group together values into regular intervals rather than on the basis of any particular value (as is done in bar charts).

Using the GSS96 data, we can produce a histogram representing the distribution of the ages of the subjects in the data.

Graphs
> *Histogram*
>> *Variable*: AGE

Although the left leg of the curve is cut off because no subjects below age 18 were interviewed in the 1996 General Social Survey, it is interesting to note how closely this histogram approximates a bell curve (Figure 5.4).

All of the options previously discussed are available in the *Chart Editor* window to refine the presentation of histograms. There are a couple of options for histograms that are especially useful, however. One option is to have SPSS construct a normal curve over the histogram. This is done with the commands:

Chart
> *Options*
>> *Display*: Normal Curve.

Another way of refining the presentation is to stipulate the number of bars to be represented in the histogram. In the case of the histogram in Figure 5.4, I allowed SPSS to automatically generate what it believes to be an appropriate number of bars. I could, however, override this function and command it to increase or decrease the number of bars, using the command:

> *Chart*
> > *Axis*
> > > *Interval*
> > > > *Intervals*: Custom.

It may be useful to take a few moments and explore the capacities of SPSS in creating and modifying histograms.

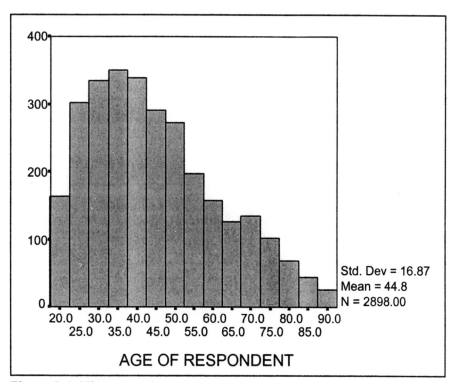

Figure 5.4 Histogram Output

Box Plots

A fourth method of graphically depicting univariate statistics is with box plots. Creating a box plot was discussed in a previous chapter as part of the *Explore* command. Recall that box plots are used in univariate analysis to examine the distributions of continuous data. To construct a box plot of the variable age (Figure 5.5), we would perform the following operations:

> *Statistics*
>> *Summarize*
>>> *Explore*
>>>> *Dependent List*: AGE
>>>> *Display*: Both.

The Chart Editor features are available for box plots and can be accessed by double clicking on the box plot generated in the Output Navigator window.

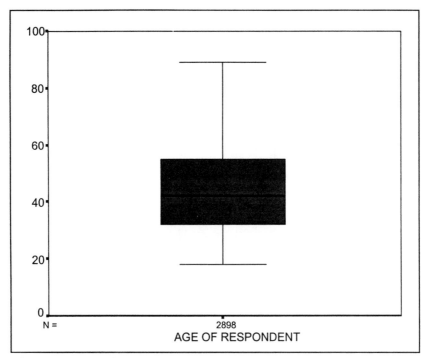

Figure 5.5 Box Plot Output

Bivariate Graphing

Bivariate graphing can show relationships between variables in a more powerful manner than is usually possible with numeric statistics. For example, bivariate graphs can show if relationships are linear or follow a curve pattern. These curves, when demonstrated, can have a profound impact on our understanding of social behavior. For instance, a classic book in environmental science, *The Limits to Growth* (Meadows 1972) is based on the implications of the curvilinear relationship between resource consumption and its environmental consequences. Were it not for the author's ability to graph these relationships, he probably would have had a much more difficult task in explaining the implications of the theory to policy makers and other scientists.

In Chapter 6 and Chapter 7, we will examine some ways to graph predicted relationships between two variables. In this chapter we will concentrate on graphing the actual values of cases in the data sets. Bar charts and box plots can graph the relationships between categorical and continuous variables. Scatter plots are designed to graph relationships between continuous variables (Table 5.2).

Table 5.2 Variable Formats and Bivariate Graphing Procedures

Graphing Technique	Variable Format
Bar charts	Categorical-Categorical
Box plots	Categorical-Continuous
Scatter plots	Continuous-Continuous

Bar Charts

Bar charts can be used to display bivariate relationships between two categorical variables. As an illustration, construct a bar chart between race (RACE) and opinion concerning the practice of giving preferential hiring of blacks (AFFRMACT). The bar chart can be effectively used to show the degree to which whites, blacks and other minorities agree or disagree with affirmative action as a social policy.

> *Graphs*
> > *Bar*
> > > *Clustered*
> > > *Data in Chart Are*: Summaries for groups of cases
> > > > *Bars Represent*: % of cases
> > > > *Category Axis*: AFFRMACT
> > > > *Define Clusters By*: RACE
> > > > > *Titles*: Opinions on Affirmative Action by Race
> > > > > (If missing values are incorporated into the graph, check *Options*.)

Again, you will observe that your bar chart looks slightly different than the one represented in Figure 5.6. You can restructure your chart by again using the *Chart Editor* window by double clicking on the graph generated in the *Output Navigator* window.

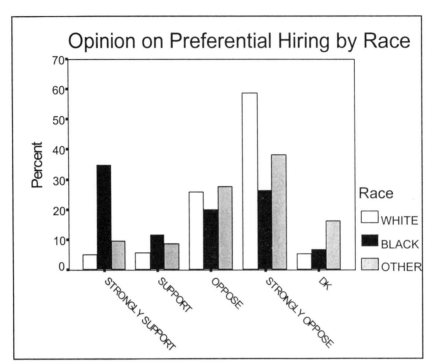

Figure 5.6 Cluster Bar Chart Output

Affirmative action, the program designed to facilitate minority entry into college education and professional jobs, has become a hot button issue in racial politics. This chart is interesting in that it poignantly demonstrates how strongly racial groups are divided on preferential hiring practices. Whites are overwhelmingly against preferences in hiring. It is interesting to observe that while nearly 40% of blacks strongly favor preferences in hiring, a considerable proportion of blacks are opposed to affirmative action as well.

Box Plots

Box plots can be used to analyze the relationship between a continuous and a categorical variable. To examine the strength of using box plots to show relationships, open the STATES data set and examine the relationship between geographic region (REGION4) and infant mortality rates (HTS348). Use the following commands to construct a box plot of these two variables:

> *Graphs*
>> *Box Plot*
>>> *Simple*
>>> *Data in Chart Are*: Summaries for groups of cases
>>>> *Variable*: HTS348
>>>> *Category Axis*: REGION4

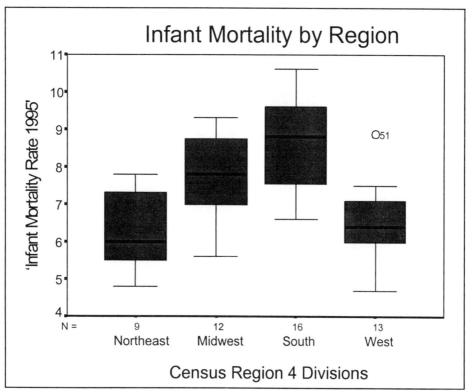

Figure 5.7 Bivariate Box Plot

It is apparent that the South and the Midwest have comparatively high infant mortality rates in comparison to the Northeast and West (Figure 5.7). An advantage of generating box plots, as opposed to simply comparing median values, is that we also gain an appreciation for the spread of values. One thing that stands out in the above box plot is that the Northeast as a whole experiences much lower infant mortality rates than the South as a whole.

Scatter Plots

Scatter plots are designed to demonstrate the relationships between two continuous variables. Using the STATES data, let us further analyze the reason why infant mortality rates are disproportionately high in the South. It is unlikely that there is something climatic causing these rates to be inflated and they are probably due to social causes. One social cause of infant mortality has to do with poverty. We can examine this relationship using the scatter plot command:

> *Graphs*
> > *Scatter*
> > > *Simple*
> > > > *Y Axis*: HTS348 (Infant Mortality Rate 1995)
> > > > *X Axis*: PVS501 (Poverty Rate 1995)
> > > > *Title*: Poverty and Infant Mortality.

In the scatter plot represented in Figure 5.8, we can observe the relationship between poverty and infant mortality. If there was no relationship, we would expect the points on the graph to be scattered randomly, much like dropping a handful of sand on a desk. However, because the points tend to pull from the lower left of the graph to the upper right, it indicates a positive association between these two variables.

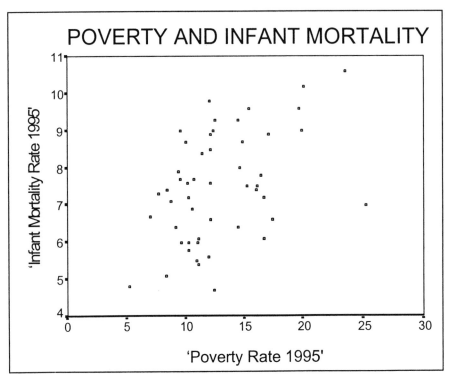

Figure 5.8 A Bivariate Scatter Plot

Summary

Graphing carries considerable persuasive power, especially when used to explain social relationships to people less versed in statistics. Graphing also displays nuances in distributions and relationships between variables which might otherwise go unnoticed. SPSS offers a wide variety of graphing techniques. This chapter has introduced some of these techniques, as well as some of the options in editing graphs using the *Chart Editor* window.

Key Terms

Chart Editor Window	Box Plots	Bar Charts
Pie Charts	Histograms	Scatter Plots

References and Further Reading

Du Toit, S. H. C.,A.G.W. Steyn, and R.H. Stumpf 1986. *Graphical Exploratory Data Analysis*. New York : Springer-Verlag.

Meadows, Donella. 1972. *The Limits to Growth*. New York: Universe Books.

Tufte, Edward. 1986. *The Visual Display of Quantitative Information*. Cheshire, Connecticut: Graphics Press.

Chapter 5 Exercises

Name_____   Date_____

1. Using the GSS96 data construct and print a pie chart displaying opinions concerning whether the government should provide housing to the poor (AIDHOUSE). Give an appropriate title to the graph and refine the graph so that it is clearly printed and aesthetically appealing. Exclude missing cases. Note, if your printer does not support color printing, you will need to change the color of the wedges. Describe this chart below.

2. Using the GSS96 data construct and print a refined graph examining the relationship between AIDHOUSE and RACE. Exclude missing cases. Do you observe a difference between race and the opinion that the government should provide housing to the poor? Describe this relationship.

3. Using the STATES data set, construct (but don't print) a histogram of ENS212 (Hazardous Waste Sites on the National Priority List Per 10K SqMi 96).   What does this graph inform us of the distribution of Hazardous Waste Sites?

4. Using the STATES data set construct, refine, and print a graph showing the distribution of hazardous waste sites (ENS212) according to the 9 Census Regions (REGION9). How could this analysis influence decision making on where to allocate funding for hazardous site clean-up?

5. Using the STATES data construct, refine, and print a graph showing the relationship between the distribution of hazardous waste sites (ENS212) and the age-adjusted death rate by cancer 1997 (HTS359). To what extent do you perceive a relationship between these two variables?

6. Test to see whether the relationship between HTS359 and ENS212 is statistically significant.

Sig.=_____

Is it significant?   Yes   No

7. Pose a hypothesis between any two variables in either the STATES or GSS96 data sets.

A. State the hypothesis:

B. Construct and print a refined univariate graph of the dependent variable.

C. Construct and print a refined bivariate graph of the relationship between these two variables.

D. Determine if the relationship is statistically significant.   Sig.=_____

                                        Is it significant?   Yes   No

E. Explain the extent to which your hypothesis is supported by your analysis.

8. Pose another hypothesis between any two variables in either the STATES or GSS96 data sets.

    A. State the hypothesis:

    B. Construct and print a refined univariate graph of the dependent variable.

    C. Construct and print a refined bivariate graph of the relationship between these two variables.

    D. Determine if the relationship is statistically significant.   Sig.=_____

                                 Is it significant?   Yes   No

    E. Explain the extent to which your hypothesis is supported by your analysis.

Chapter 6
Multivariate Analysis: Regression

Overview

In Chapter 4 and Chapter 5 we examined common methods for testing the relationships between two variables. Many research projects, however, require testing the influence of multiple factors on the dependent variable. This is the task of multivariate analysis and there are a number of advantages to engaging in these statistical procedures. One strength is that multivariate techniques allow the researcher to control for the influence of potentially spurious factors. Because we can load multiple variables into the statistical model, the influence of each variable is taken into account. This enables the researcher to address questions such as:

Do African American students do as well in college as White students if differences in family incomes are taken into account?

Do male and female college professors make the same level of income if we control for their level of professional accomplishment?

If we control for the differences in age of the population of each state, is health care equitably funded in the United States?

The practice of examining the potentials for spurious relationships is termed **controlling for extraneous factors** and multivariate analysis is suited to this purpose.

Another advantage of multivariate analysis is that it enables researchers to test the cumulative impact multiple independent variables level on a dependent variable. Bivariate analysis is suited to **nomothetic analysis**, the analysis of the influence of a single variable on a dependent variable. Multivariate analysis is well suited to **ideographic analysis**, an approach which endeavors to provide a full description of how social behavior is influenced by multiple factors. Some questions open to ideographic analysis include:

What are the main factors which contribute to welfare dependency?

To what extent do education and family background play in influencing a person's economic success?

What are the main factors which influence a person's propensity to engage in family violence?

In this chapter and Chapter 7, you will learn how to produce and interpret output from two types of multivariate analytic procedures using SPSS, OLS regression, and logistic regression. The mathematical procedures involved in OLS regression and logistic regression are much more sophisticated than those of bivariate statistical procedures. Again, we will not be so much concerned with how these numbers are produced (we'll leave that task to SPSS), but rather with how to interpret the statistics generated.

The Regression Equation: A Bivariate Example

Regression refers to ordinary least squares (OLS) regression. The calculations underpinning a regression equation are designed to find a formula which best approximates the linear relationship between two or more variables. In this capacity, regression can be thought of as working much like a correlation coefficient. However, regression opens up another advantage to the researcher by creating a statistic that indicates the degree of change in the dependent variable that is associated with a one unit change in the independent variable. As a consequence, we can numerically or graphically map the predicted relationship of the dependent variable with any value of the independent variable.

Using the STATES data, let's examine the degree to which poverty rates influence teenage birth rates using *regression*. Our guiding hypothesis is that states with higher poverty rates will tend to have higher teenage birth rates.

Statistics
> *Regression*
> > *Linear*
> > > *Dependent Variable*: HTS339 (Teenage Birth Rate/1000 1994)
> > > *Independent Variable*: PVS501 (Poverty Rate 1995)

Model Summary[a,b]

Model	Variables Entered	Removed	R	R Square	Adjusted R Square	Std. Error of the Estimate
1	PVS501 'Poverty Rate 1995'[c,d]		.700	.490	.479	11.8899

a. Dependent Variable: HTS339 'Teenage Birth Rate 1994'

b. Method: Enter

c. Independent Variables: (Constant), PVS501 'Poverty Rate 1995'

d. All requested variables entered.

ANOVA[a]

Model		Sum of Squares	df	Mean Square	F	Sig.
1	Regression	6652.374	1	6652.374	47.057	.000[b]
	Residual	6927.071	49	141.369		
	Total	13579.4	50			

a. Dependent Variable: HTS339 'Teenage Birth Rate 1994'

b. Independent Variables: (Constant), PVS501 'Poverty Rate 1995'

Coefficients[a]

Model		Unstandardized Coefficients		Standardized Coefficients		
		B	Std. Error	Beta	t	Sig.
1	(Constant)	20.593	5.411		3.806	.000
	PVS501 'Poverty Rate 1995'	2.691	.392	.700	6.860	.000

a. Dependent Variable: HTS339 'Teenage Birth Rate 1994'

Figure 6.1 Regression Output

In reading the regression output, reproduced in Figure 6.1, the first thing I look for is whether there is a statistically significant relationship between these two variables. Examining the row for "Poverty Rate/1000 1995" in the Coefficients Table, I find a significance (Sig.) score of .000. This is a statistically significant relationship.

The next question concerns the strength and direction of that relationship. This information is also found in the Coefficients Table, in the column for Unstandardized Coefficients B. This regression coefficient refers to the slope of the regression line. The slope indicates the amount of change in the dependent variable (Y) which is associated with a one unit change in the independent variable (X). The coefficient (B) in this regression for "Poverty Rate/1000 1995" is 2.691. This indicates that for every 1% increase in the poverty rate, we can expect a 2.691 increase in the teenage birth rate.

A third question regression is able to address relates to the **R Square** statistic. The R Square indicates the degree to which the statistical model explains variation in the dependent variable. In other words, the R Square indicates how much of the fluctuation in the dependent variable is produced by the independent variable(s). If an R Square of 1.00 is generated, it indicates that 100% of the variance in the dependent variable is explained by the independent variables. Conversely, an R Square of 0.0 would indicate that none of the variance in the dependent variable is explained by the independent variables. In the case of the regression of the poverty rate on teen birth rate, we find an R Square of .490 in the Model Summary Table. This indicates that 49% of the variance in the teen birth rate from state to state can be explained by variations in the poverty rates. Poverty is not only a statistically significant factor related to teen births, it alone can explain almost half of the variation in teen birth rates!

Regression is also well suited to graphing techniques because it involves finding an equation which can produce a line which best estimates the relationship between two or more variables. This graph line is produced with the equation $\hat{Y}=A+B(X)$ and uses the output of the regression coefficients.

$\hat{Y}$	=	A	+	B	(X)
Predicted	=	Y axis	+	predicted increase	Multiply
Value of Y		intercept		of Y for 1 unit	value of X
(Dependent		(The constant)		increase in X	(Independent
Variable)				(The slope)	Variable)

Recall that the regression coefficient (B) is termed the **slope**. The slope (B) is a measure of how much change in Y can be predicted with every one unit increase in X (the independent variable). In this case, because we are concerned with predicting the increases in teenage birth rate, B indicates how much that rate increases for every one unit increase in the poverty rate. In interpreting the above regression output, we found a slope (B) of 2.691. For every percent increase in the poverty rate, we observe a 2.691 increase in the teen birth rate. Any regression line can be graphed so long as the researcher knows the slope and one other piece of information, the **constant**. The constant is that point at which the regression line is predicted to touch the Y axis (or in other words the predicted value of Y when X=0). In the above regression output, you can find the constant in the Coefficients Table in the first row of the column Unstandardized Coefficients B (20.593).

Incidentally, SPSS can give you these predicted values to enable you to graph them using the

Scatterplot command. When you run the *Regression* command, select *Save* and save the *Predicted Values* as Unstandardized.

> *Statistics*
> > *Regression*
> > > *Linear.*
> > > > *Dependent Variable*: HTS339 (Teenage Birth Rate/1000 1994)
> > > > *Independent Variable*: PVS501 (Poverty Rate 1995)
> > > > *Save*
> > > > > *Predicted Values*: Unstandardized

This will create a new variable in your data set "PRE_1," the prediction of teenage birth rate for every case in your data set. To graph these predicted values, use the *Scatterplot* command, and select PVS501 as the X axis variable and PRE_1 as the Y axis variable (Figure 6.2):

> *Graphs*
> > *Scatter*
> > > *Simple*
> > > > *X Axis*: PVS501
> > > > *Y Axis*: PRE_1.

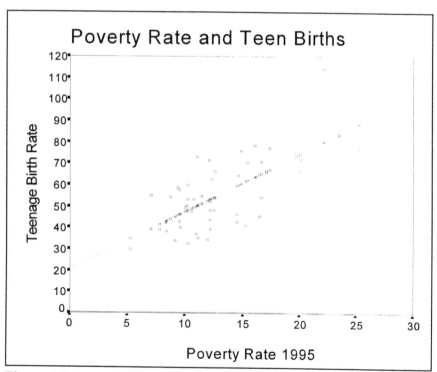

Figure 6.2 Scatter Plot with Regression Line

Graphing relationships is a powerful way of examining regressions. However, it isn't always necessary. Suppose we wanted to know what the predicted teen birth rate would be if the poverty rate is 25%. One solution would be to graph the relationship and manually trace this value. Another solution would be to use the regression equation $\hat{Y}=A+B(X)$.

$\hat{Y}$	$=$	A	$+$	B	(X)
Predicted	$=$	20.593	$+$	2.691	(25)

$\hat{Y}$	$=$	A	$+$	B	(X)
87.868	$=$	20.593	$+$	2.691	(25)

By using the slope, the constant, and the selected value of X (the poverty rate), we are able to quickly calculate that a state with a poverty rate of 25% will have a predicted teenage birth rate of 87.868/1000 teenage women.

Data and Multivariate Regression

Multivariate regression operates on the same principles as bivariate regression. Coefficients are read in the same manner, as well as significance tests. As discussed above, multiple regression offers the advantage of allowing the researcher to examine the impact of multiple variables acting in conjunction with one another on the dependent variable. Before generating and analyzing the regression coefficients, it is imperative to understand the process of selecting variables for the multivariate analysis.

If multiple regression works so well to detect relationships, one might suspect that the most efficient manner of analyzing data would be to load all of the variables in the data set into a regression to observe which have significant associations with the dependent variable. While this may seem an appealing (albeit lazy) approach, it suffers from a problem relating to **degrees of freedom**. Degrees of freedom refers to the number of scores in a sample that are "free to vary." It is a means of compensating for the possibility of drawing inaccurate conclusions from a sample to the population. The more a sample is free to vary, the lower the criteria will be to attain statistical significance. This means that it is easier for a researcher to attain statistically significant relationships when s/he has many degrees of freedom. With each loss of a degree of freedom, the higher the standards will be for statistical significance to be asserted. The reason for not loading variables indiscriminately is that each new variable added to a regression equation reduces the degrees of freedom by one. In selecting variables for multivariate analysis, it is in the researcher's interest to be highly selective in determining which variables to include in the statistical model. Therefore, the selection of variables in a regression should be hypothesis driven.

It is also important to select independent variables which reasonably vary from one another. When variables are strongly correlated they are said to be **collinear**. If variables are collinear, there is not enough variation between these variables for the multivariate regression procedure to operate correctly. For example, it would be against my interests to perform a multivariate analysis which included two strongly associated independent variables which measure essentially the same thing, such as the percent of the population living below the poverty line (PVS501) and the percent of school age children living in poverty (PVS502). These are two different variables, but they are so strongly collinear (correlation of .94) that they do not really vary sufficiently from one another to be distinguishable in the regression equation. Collinear variables often result in peculiar outcomes in regression output. In the case of the above two variables and their relationship to teenage birth rate, we would assume that because both poverty variables are strongly associated with one another that both would be significantly related to the teen birth rate. However, if we run a multivariate regression of PVS501 and PVS502 on teen birth rate (HTS339), PVS502 fails to become statistically significant (even though it would be in a bivariate regression). The implications are that researchers should be careful to avoid putting collinear variables in regression equations. To check for collinearity, the independent variables can be regressed upon one another. If a strong regression emerges from this test, it is possible that collinearity is influencing the original regression output. If collinearity is identified as a problem, variables may need to be analyzed in separate regression equations.

OLS regression operates on the assumption that the independent and dependent variable distributions conform to a **normal distribution**. While it is reasonable to include some dichotomous independent variables in the regression equation, the more variables included which are nonnormal, the less confidence we can place on the output accurately representing the relationship between the independent and dependent variables.

Regression requires that the dependent variable be in the form of **continuous data**. Regression expects the independent variables to be continuous as well. For example, regression cannot analyze the impact of race when race is categorically coded as "Black," "White," "Hispanic," and "Asian." If there are categorical independent variables, such as race, it is tolerable to construct **dummy variables** in order to examine their impact on the dependent variable. Dummy variables take the form of binary variables, where one category is coded as "1" and the other as "0." The conventional practice in constructing dummy variables is to code the comparison group as "1" and the reference group as "0." In the case of race, a dummy variable could be produced by recoding "White" to the value "1" and "Nonwhite" (all other racial categories) to "0." The dummy variable regression coefficients should be interpreted with caution and graphing the relationships can be helpful in making accurate interpretations. In the case of race as a dummy variable, it can be used to determine if being white, in comparison to all other racial groups combined, has an effect on the dependent variable in question. The researcher could then produce another dummy variable indicating "Black" (1) versus all other racial groups (0), and test the relationships for African Americans.

Multiple regression can be greatly influenced by an observation, or small set of observations, which "pull" the equation away from the general pattern of the relationship. These influential cases are sometimes termed "outliers." **Outliers** are atypical cases and can exert great influence on the regression output. If there is an exceptional case in the data, having atypical high or low values, one solution is to drop that case from the regression analysis and report the influence of that case in the text of the report. For example, because Nevada has a high divorce rate because of its laws, it is often excluded from regressions of state level data examining the social causes of divorce because it exerts undue influence on the regressions.

OLS regression expects a **linear relationship** between each independent variable and the dependent variable. Curvilinear relationships are not anticipated by the regression equation because the equation expects a constant change between the independent variables and the dependent variable. To check for linearity, it is often useful to perform bivariate scatter plots of each independent variable on the dependent variable. This will reveal how variables are related, as well as identify outliers.

Finally, the OLS regression can only measure the effects of variables included in the equation. Even though multiple variables may be included in the statistical model, it is still possible to have spurious relationships if important variables are left out of the model. It is always possible that some omitted variable causes spurious findings.

These are a few of the concerns which the careful researcher should be advised to examine before making hasty conclusions based on regression coefficients. One of the best ways to address each of these concerns is to approach the data analysis in the systematic manner outlined in this book. Engaging in univariate analysis will reveal potential problems of outliers, nonnormal distributions, and determine whether data are continuous or categorical. Bivariate analysis, the next stage of data analysis, reveals bivariate relationships, whether these relationships are linear, and potential collinear relationships between variables. Once these tasks are accomplished, the researcher is in a good position to engage in multivariate analysis. While the above concerns may seem daunting, on the bright side OLS regression is often described as a "robust" statistical procedure. It is said to be robust, or strong, because it can tolerate moderate breaches between the data and the expectations described above.

Multivariate Regression: An Example

Let us expand our study of teenage birth rate (HTS339) into a multivariate analysis. My interest is in examining the causes of teenage births and testing the relationships frequently forwarded in the popular press.

I will test the following hypotheses:

Ho1. Teenage Birth Rate is positively associated with poverty.
   Independent Variable: PVS501

Ho2. Teenage Birth Rate is negatively associated with expenditures per pupil.
   Independent Variable: SCS142

Ho3. Teenage Birth Rate is positively associated with the unemployment rate.
   Independent Variable: JBS170

Ho4. Teenage Birth Rate is positively associated with the amount of welfare (AFDC)
     a family receives.
   Independent Variable: PVS531

One advantage of loading these variables together into a multiple regression equation is that we are able to look at the simultaneous influence of all of these factors, as well as control for the influence of one variable on another. For example, conservative social theory suggests that welfare acts as a motivation for teenagers to have babies (Murray 1984). The argument is that these young mothers are essentially rewarded for behaviors which should be discouraged. On the other hand, liberal social theory suggests that it is primarily education, poverty, and lack of opportunities which cause teenage births (Wilson 1987). This multivariate regression accounts for the potential influence of all these factors.

To run this regression, use the following commands:

Statistics
  Regression
    Linear
      Dependent Variable: HST339 (Teenage Birth Rate/1000 1994)
      Independent Variable: PVS501 (Poverty Rate 1995)
             SCS142 (Expenditures per Pupil 1996)
             JBS170 (Unemployment Rate 1996)
             PVS531 (Average Monthly AFDC Payment 1995)

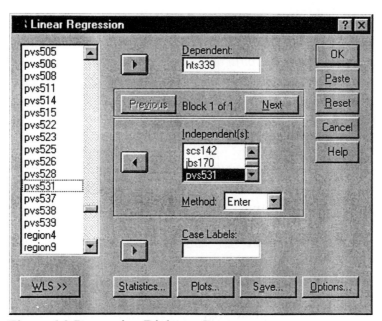

Figure 6.3 Regression Dialogue Box

The result of this regression is compelling (Figure 6.4). We will interpret this regression equation in the same manner as we did the bivariate regression by first looking at the significance tests, then the regression coefficients, and finally the R Square value.

Regression

Model Summary[a,b]

Model	Variables Entered	Variables Removed	R	R Square	Adjusted R Square	Std. Error of the Estimate
1	PVS531 'Avg Monthly AFDC Payment per Recipient Family 1995', JBS170 Unemployment Rate 1996, SCS142 Expenditures per Pupil in Elem and Sec Schools 1996, PVS501 'Poverty Rate 1995'[c,d]		.817	.668	.639	9.8996

a. Dependent Variable: HTS339 'Teenage Birth Rate 1994'

b. Method: Enter

c. Independent Variables: (Constant), PVS531 'Avg Monthly AFDC Payment per Recipient Family 1995', JBS170 Unemployment Rate 1996, SCS142 Expenditures per Pupil in Elem and Sec Schools 1996, PVS501 'Poverty Rate 1995'

d. All requested variables entered.

ANOVA[a]

Model		Sum of Squares	df	Mean Square	F	Sig.
1	Regression	9071.347	4	2267.837	23.141	.000[b]
	Residual	4508.098	46	98.002		
	Total	13579.4	50			

a. Dependent Variable: HTS339 'Teenage Birth Rate 1994'

b. Independent Variables: (Constant), PVS531 'Avg Monthly AFDC Payment per Recipient Family 1995', JBS170 Unemployment Rate 1996, SCS142 Expenditures per Pupil in Elem and Sec Schools 1996, PVS501 'Poverty Rate 1995'

Coefficients^a

Model		Unstandardized Coefficients		Standardized Coefficients	t	Sig.
		B	Std. Error	Beta		
1	(Constant)	39.493	9.800		4.030	.000
	PVS501 'Poverty Rate 1995'	.826	.499	.215	1.653	.105
	SCS142 Expenditures per Pupil in Elem and Sec Schools 1996	-3.5E-03	.002	-.263	-2.173	.035
	JBS170 Unemployment Rate 1996	7.604	1.694	.545	4.488	.000
	PVS531 'Avg Monthly AFDC Payment per Recipient Family 1995'	-3.5E-02	.014	-.282	-2.494	.016

a. Dependent Variable: HTS339 'Teenage Birth Rate 1994'

Figure 6.4 Multivariate Regression Output

In scanning through the significance tests in the Coefficients Table, we find that all of these variables are significant except PVS501(sig.=.105). This variable just barely fails to reach significance. There are a few possible explanations of why this variable may not have reached significance in the multivariate equation, even though it was shown to be strongly associated with the teenage birth rate in the bivariate regression. One possibility is that the reduction in the degrees of freedom essentially raised the threshold of this variable attaining statistical significance. Another possibility is that collinearity is present between this variable and another independent variable. You can check this potentiality by producing a correlation matrix of the independent variables using the *correlate* command. The highest correlation of PVS501 with any other variable is .49. While this is a fairly strong correlation, there is probably enough variation between variables to rule out collinearity as a cause of the loss of statistical significance.

A third possibility exists, which involves trusting the multiple regression output. The implications are that it is not so much concentrations of poverty which influence the teenage birth rate, but rather the other variables in the equation which influence fluctuations in the teen birth rates. I would suggest the following may be a more appropriate interpretation of this variable. Teenage birth rates are influenced by the amount of poverty in a state, but only modestly so. The other variables have a much greater impact on how many teens have babies. Hypothesis 1 is modestly supported.

Hypothesis 2 predicts that the more a state expends on a pupil, the lower the teenage birth rate will be. The Coefficients Table supports this hypothesis and the relationship is statistically significant

(Sig.=.035). The regression coefficient for variable SCS142 is -3.5E-03. Changing this coefficient to natural numbers produces a coefficient of -.0035. Using this coefficient as a slope informs us that for every $1 spent per pupil, we can expect a decline in the teenage birth rate by .0035/1000. This does not sound like much, but how much would you expect one dollar to buy in changing behavior? If we multiply this times 1000, we would be able to predict how much an increase $1000 funding per student would affect the teen birth rate. For every $1000 spent on students per year, we could expect 3.5 fewer births per 1000 teenage girls.

Hypothesis 3 asserts that the higher the unemployment rate, the higher the teenage birth rate. Again, this hypothesis is supported. Examining the Coefficient Table we find the regression coefficient is 7.604, and it is statistically significant (Sig.=.000). When we control for the other variables in this equation, this coefficient indicates that a 1% increase in the unemployment rate results in 7.6 more births per 1000 teenage girls.

Hypothesis 4 predicts that the more a state spends on welfare per recipient family, the higher the teenage birth rate will be. We find this is a statistically significant relationship (Sig.= .016). However, the negative regression coefficient indicates a relationship opposite the one predicted in the hypothesis. The more a state spends on welfare per recipient family *the lower the teenage birth rate*. Again, we can convert the coefficient B (-3.5E-02) to the natural number -.035. This indicates that for every $1 that a state gives a family in AFDC payments each month, the teenage birth rate will decline by .035 births per 1000 teenagers. If we multiply this times 250, we can predict how much an increase in $250 expenditures per welfare family per month will "buy" in decreasing the teenage birth rate, controlling for all other factors. An increase in AFDC payments of $250 will theoretically decrease the teenage birth rate by 8.75 births per 1000 teenagers.

While the liberal-conservative debate concerning social policy and social behavior cannot be settled with one regression and one set of data, these data seem to offer much stronger support for liberal theories concerning the causes of teenage births. Based on this analysis, teenage birth rate can be lowered by increasing expenditures on AFDC, increasing the amount spent on students, and decreasing poverty rates. In fact, if we look at the R Square statistic in the Model Summary Table, we find that 67% (R Square=.668) of the variation in the teenage birth rate can be attributed to these four variables.

Graphing a Multivariate Regression

Graphing a relationship revealed through multivariate regression requires using the *compute* command and the regression equation. By using the output of the multivariate regression, we can produce a regression line which predicts a relationship of the dependent variable to a single independent variable. This requires designating specific parameters for all of the remaining independent variables.

The multivariate regression equation is similar to the bivariate regression equation, only extended:

$$\hat{Y} = A + B_1(X_1) + B_2(X_2) + B_3(X_3) + B_4(X_4)......$$

$\hat{Y}$=Predicted Value of the dependent variable
A=Constant
B_1=Slope of Variable 1 X_1=Chosen value of Variable 1
B_2=Slope of Variable 2 X_2=Chosen value of Variable 2
B_3=Slope of Variable 3 X_3=Chosen value of Variable 3
B_4=Slope of Variable 4 X_4=Chosen value of Variable 4

In order to produce the graphic regression line, we will need to calculate a new variable which contains all of the above information. I am interested in graphically depicting the influence of AFDC payments on the teenage birth rate, so I will compute a new variable (BIRTHPD), controlling for all of the factors aside from the variable indicating AFDC payments (PVS531). I could set these values at any level, but I have decided to set all of them at their mean value (which I generated using Summarize). To generate these needed values, input the following equation into the *Compute* command to generate the new variable BIRTHPD and label the variable "Predicted Teen Birth Rate."

Transform
    Compute
        Target Variable: BIRTHPD
        Numeric Expression: 39.493+(.862*13.12)+(-.0035*5616.84)+(7.604*4.86)+
                          (-.035*PVS531)
        Type and Label: Predicted Teen Birth Rate

Sources of numbers in the above equation.
    Constant (A)= 39.493

Variable	B	Mean Value
PVS501	.862	13.12
SCS142	-.0035	5616.84
JBS170	7.604	4.86
PVS531	-.035	PVS531

The new variable BIRTHPD predicts the teen birth rate for all of the states at the various levels of AFDC payments/month (Figure 6.5). It holds constant the other variables at their mean values. To graph this relationship, use the scatterplot command (Figure 6.6):

Graphs
    Scatter
        Simple
            Y Axis: BIRTHPD
            X Axis: PVS531.

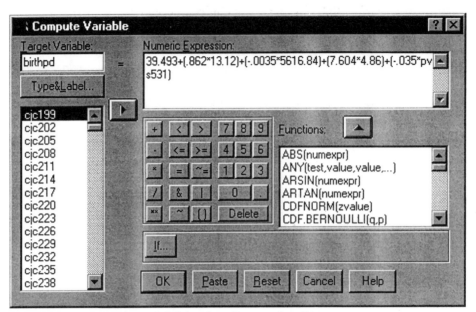

Figure 6.5 Computing a Multivariate Regression Line

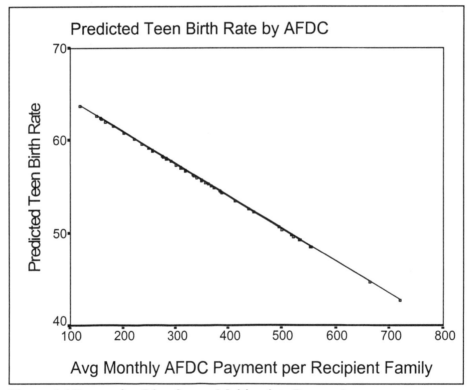

Figure 6.6 Regression Line from a Multivariate Regression

Summary

SPSS is able to process multivariate procedures such as ordinary least squares regression. Regression is a powerful statistical tool because it enables researchers to analyze the cumulative impact of many variables, as well as control for extraneous factors. While regression is a robust statistical procedure, it is important to understand and abide by the assumptions under which regression operates. This includes avoiding circumstances where variables may be collinear, being selective of which variables to include in the equation, and assuring that the relationship is linear.

Key Terms

Extraneous Factors	Nomothetic Analysis	Ideographic Analysis
R Square	Slope	Degrees of Freedom
Collinearity	Dummy Variables	Outliers
Linear Relationship	Constant	

References and Further Reading

Grimm, Laurence and Paul Yarnold. 1995. *Reading and Understanding Multivariate Statistics*. Washington, D.C.:American Psychological Society.

Hamilton, Lawrence. 1990. *Modern Data Analysis*. Pacific Grove, California: Brooks/Cole Publishing.

Levin, Jack and James Fox. 1997. *Elementary Statistics in Social Research*. Longman: New York.

Murray, Charles. 1984. *Losing Ground: American Social Policy, 1950-1980*. New York: Basic Books.

Sen, Ashish and Muni Srivastava. 1990. *Regression Analysis: Theory, Methods and Applications*. New York: Springer-Verlag.

Tarbach, Barbara and Linda Fidell. 1983. *Using Multivariate Statistics*. Harper and Row: New York.

Wilson, William Julius. 1987. *The Truly Disadvantaged*. Chicago: University of Chicago Press.

Chapter 6 Exercises

Name_____   Date_____

1. Using the STATES data, test the hypothesis that states which are predominantly black receive lower educational funding. Test this hypothesis by performing a bivariate linear regression on SCS142 (Expenditures per Pupil in Elementary and Secondary Schools 1996) and DMS451 (Percent of Population Black 1995). Fill in the following statistics:

Regression Coefficient B for DMS451   _____

Significance   _____

Is the relationship significant?   Yes   No

R Square   _____

In your own words, describe the relationship between SCS142 and DMS451. How would you explain these findings?

2. Using the STATES data set, examine the relationship between the AIDS death rate (HTS384) and the percent of the population of a state that is urban (DMS439).

Regression Coefficient B for DMS439   _____

Significance   _____

Is the relationship significant?   Yes   No

R Square   _____   _____

In your own words, describe the relationship between HTS384 and DMS439. How would you explain these findings?

3. Graph the regression line between the AIDS death rate (HTS384) and the percent of the population of a state that is urban (DMS439). To perform this task, follow these procedures:

Statistics
> *Regression*
>> *Linear*
>>> *Dependent*: HTS384
>>> *Independent*: DMS439
>>> *Save*: Predicted Values Unstandardized

This will generate the predicted values for your regression line. If this is the first time you have predicted a value during this session, your new variable will be called PRE_1. Note, if you have generated other predicted values, your predicted value may have a different numeric designator, such as PRE_2 or PRE_3. If this is the case, substitute in the graph commands the most recent prediction.

Graphs
> *Scatter*
>> *Overlay*
>>> *Y-X Pairs*: HTS384 DMS439
>>> PRE_1   DMS439

Print the graph.
Offer your interpretation of the regression line in relationship to the scatter plot graph. Do you think the regression coefficient accurately reflects the relationship between the percent of the population which is urban and the AIDS death rate?

4. Perform a multivariate regression to determine if social stress influences the rape rate (CRC348). Include as indicators of potential social stress the percentage of the population that is urban (DMS439), the divorce rate (DMS492), and the unemployment rate (JBS170).

Constant   _____

R Square   _____

Regression Coefficient B for DMS439   _____

Significance   _____

Is the relationship significant?   Yes   No

Regression Coefficient B for DMS492   _____

Significance   _____

Is the relationship significant?   Yes   No

Regression Coefficient B for JBS170   _____

Significance   _____

Is the relationship significant?   Yes   No

In your own words, describe these relationships and whether the theory that social stress influences the rape rate is supported by these statistics.

5. Using the output from the above regression of social stress and the rape rate, write below the formula which would be used to generate a graph line showing the influence of the divorce rate on the rape rate. Hold constant DMS439 and JBS170 at their mean values. You will need to generate the mean values using the *Summarize - Descriptives* command.

$$\hat{Y} \quad = \quad A \quad + \quad B_1(X_1) \quad + \quad B_2(X_2) \quad + \quad B_3(X_3)$$

6. Compute a new variable "RAPE2" using the above equation. Label RAPE2 "Predicted Rape Rate 2." Graph and print relationship using the command:

    Graph
        Scatter
            Simple
                Y Axis: RAPE2
                X Axis: DMS492

7. Using the output from the above regression of social stress and the rape rate, write below the formula which would be used to generate a graph line showing the influence of the urban population on the rape rate. Hold constant DMS492 and JBS170 at their mean values. You will need to generate the mean values using the *Summarize - Descriptives* command.

$$\hat{Y} \quad = \quad A \quad + \quad B_1(X_1) \quad + \quad B_2(X_2) \quad + \quad B_3(X_3)$$

8. Compute a new variable "RAPE3" using the above equation. Label RAPE3 "Predicted Rape Rate 3" Graph and print relationship using the command:

> *Graph*
> > *Scatter*
> > > *Simple*
> > > > *Y Axis*: RAPE3
> > > > *X Axis*: DMS439

Chapter 7
Multivariate Analysis: Logistic Regression

Overview

In the previous chapter you learned how to perform and analyze data using OLS regression. In this chapter you will learn how to analyze data using logistic regression, another powerful method of analyzing multivariate relationships. Logistic regression is similar to OLS regression in that it enables researchers to analyze the impact of multiple variables on a dependent variable. However, it differs from regression in regard to expectations about the data and in the manner in which coefficients are interpreted.

Logistic Regression

Logistic regression, sometimes referred to as logit, is similar to regression in many ways. It enables researchers to load multiple variables together in order to examine the cumulative influence of these variables on a dependent variable. It also enables the researcher to control for the influence of extraneous factors. Logistic regression is different from regression, though, in that it requires different types of data and is suited to a subtly different type of research question. Whereas regression seeks to measure the degree of influence variables have on a dependent variable, logistic regression seeks to determine the odds that an event will or will not occur. Some questions appropriate to logistic regression include:

What are the odds that a white male, married at age 33, will be divorced by the time he is 50?

What is the likelihood that a couple, married 10 years with children, will engage in frequent verbal aggression against each other?

What are the odds that violent felons will be reincarcerated within 5 years of release from their first prison sentence?

One of the most crucial differences between regression and logistic regression relates to the dependent variable. In logistic regression, the dependent variable must be framed as a **binary variable**. In other words, all of the values in the dependent variable must be polarized into the form of yes or no; occurs or does not occur; present or absent. All of these qualitative values would be represented numerically as 1 or 0. For instance, cancer diagnoses would constitute a binary variable in that biopsies come back either as positive or negative. The "positive" diagnosis in this binary variable would be coded as "1," negative results would be coded "0." The question "Have you ever been divorced?" can be coded as a binary variable because a person would be forced to answer either "yes" (1) or "no" (0). While the dependent variable in a logistic regression equation must be constructed into the form of a binary, the independent variables must be in the form of continuous variables and dummy variables.

It is possible to recode continuous variables into binary variables. For instance, alcohol consumption is often measured by asking subjects "How many drinks do you usually have in a typical day?" This will produce a wide range of responses and provide continuous data which may be suited to OLS regression. If our interest is in determining the likelihood that an individual will be an alcoholic, given personal and social factors influencing that individual, we may desire to use logistic regression. In order to use logistic regression, we would need to recode the data so that the drinking variable becomes binary, distinguishing alcoholics from nonalcoholics. The criteria should be set at a level which corresponds with the concept of the alcoholism and the data can be recoded using the *Compute* command.

Another important distinction between logistic regression and OLS regression is the difference in expectations about the relationships encountered. Recall that OLS regression anticipates linear relationships, which asserts a constant change between the dependent and independent variables. Logistic regression anticipates **sigmoidal** or **S curve** relationships rather than linear relationships. In a sigmoidal relationship, the probabilities of an event occurring change at smaller increments as the values of the independent variable reach their high and low values.

This nonlinear relationship presents a challenge to interpreting the logistic regression coefficients. Notice in Figure 7.1 that a one unit change in the variable on the X axis will produce a larger or smaller change in the Y axis, depending on the location of that one unit change. This curvilinear relationship is predicted using logarithmic functions, which in turn make it more difficult to gain an immediate understanding of the logistic regression coefficient in comparison to an OLS regression coefficient. Once the log odds are translated back to an odds ratio, using exponential mathematics, the logistic regression coefficient can be readily understood.

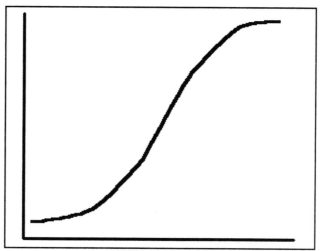

Figure 7.1 Sigmoid (S) Curve

The logistic regression equation is very similar to the OLS regression equation:

<table>
<tr><td><u>OLS Regression</u></td><td><u>Logistic Regression</u></td></tr>
<tr><td>$\hat{Y}=A+B(X)$</td><td>$\hat{G}=A+B(X)$</td></tr>
</table>

SPSS will be able to calculate the constant term (A) and the logistic regression coefficient (B). X constitutes any selected value of the independent variable. We can use these statistics to generate $\hat{G}$, the predicted log of the odds. By recalculating the log of the odds using exponential functions (explained below), we can find the probability of any event occurring if we specify the parameters of the independent variables in the same manner as in regression analysis.

Logistic regression: A Bivariate Example

A real world example will help to clarify how to interpret logistic regression coefficients. Divorce is ripe for logistic regression analysis because the divorce variable is readily constructed into binary form (1=divorced, 0=not divorced).

While we could load in any number of factors which can influence divorce, let's begin by examining how children influence the likelihood of a person ever having been divorced or separated. The guiding hypothesis is that the fewer children a person has, the less likely s/he will have ever been divorced or separated due to increased family social attachment. We will use the GSS96.SAV data to analyze this hypothesis.

The first step involves constructing a new binomial variable which distinguishes the divorced and separated respondents from those who are married or widowed (Figure 7.2 and 7.3). In order to do this correctly, you must first examine how the original variable DIVORCE is distributed and coded using the *Frequencies* and *Utilities* commands. In the frequencies output we find that one person responded DK (Doesn't Know). This value will need to be recoded in the new variable DIVORCE2 as SYSMIS (system missing). Label the new variable as "Divorced Binomial." Double check your recoded variable DIVORCE2 to make sure that it appropriately corresponds with DIVORCE. All values should either be 0 or 1 and divorced respondents should have the value 1.

Step 1: Code the dependent variable to be binary

> *Frequencies*
>> *Variables*: DIVORCE
>
> *Utilities*
>> *Variables*: DIVORCE
>
> *Transform*
>> *Recode*
>>> *Into Different Variable*: DIVORCE ->DIVORCE2
>>> *Old and New Values*:2->0
>>>> 1->1
>>>> 0->SYSMIS
>>>> 8->SYSMIS

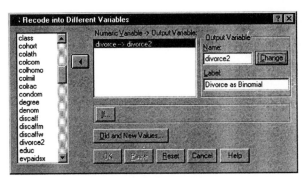

Figure 7.2 Recode Dialogue Box 1

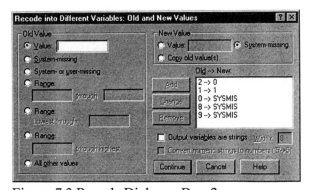

Figure 7.3 Recode Dialogue Box 2

After the dependent variable is structured into binary form, we are ready to perform the logistic regression. Logistic regression requires that at least one of the independent variables is a continuous variable. In this case, we will examine the relationship of DIVORCE2 to CHILDS (Number of Children).

Step 2: Perform the logistic regression.

> *Statistics*
> > *Regression*
> > > *Logistic*
> > > > *Dependent*: DIVORCE2
> > > > *Covariates*: CHILDS
> > > > *Save*
> > > > > *Predicted Values*: Probabilities

We will read the logistic regression output in a manner similar to that used in interpreting regression output (Figure 7.4). The first step is to see if the hypothesized relationship is statistically significant. We find that the variable CHILDS is significantly associated with divorce (Sig = .0002). By examining the logistic regression coefficient (B) we find a positive association between CHILDS and DIVORCE2 (B=.1290). The hypothesis is rejected because the greater the number of children produces a higher likelihood of experiencing divorce or separation.

The coefficient (B) is more difficult to interpret beyond this point, however, unless we graph the relationship or perform additional calculations. This is because B represents the log of the odds that a divorce will occur. It is the log values which enables SPSS to model the sigmoidal curve, which unfortunately makes the coefficient more difficult to initially interpret.

The next step is to graph this relationship. When we ran the logistic regression, we asked SPSS to save the predicted probabilities. These can be graphed in the same manner as they were graphed in regression. Your data set now has a new variable PRE_1 (the predicted values) saved. We need to perform a scatter plot of these values against CHILDS to more fully understand the dynamics of this relationship.

> *Graph*
> > *Scatterplot*
> > > *Simple*
> > > > *Y Axis*: PRE_1
> > > > *X Axis*: CHILDS

Logistic Regression

```
          Total number of cases:        2904 (Unweighted)
          Number of selected cases:     2904
          Number of unselected cases: 0
          Number of selected cases:                2904
          Number rejected because of missing data: 1256
          Number of cases included in the analysis: 1648
```

Dependent Variable Encoding:

```
Original        Internal
Value           Value
     .00        0
    1.00        1
```

Dependent Variable..   DIVORCE2   Divorce as Binomial

Beginning Block Number 0. Initial Log Likelihood Function

-2 Log Likelihood   1794.1092

* Constant is included in the model.

Beginning Block Number 1. Method: Enter

Variable(s) Entered on Step Number
1..   CHILDS   NUMBER OF CHILDREN

Estimation terminated at iteration number 3 because
Log Likelihood decreased by less than .01 percent.

```
 -2 Log Likelihood        1780.197
 Goodness of Fit          1647.185

                      Chi-Square      df Significance

 Model Chi-Square         13.912       1       .0002
 Improvement              13.912       1       .0002
```

Classification Table for DIVORCE2
```
                      Predicted
                     .00    1.00    Percent Correct
                      0  I   1
Observed             +------+------+
   .00        0    I 1262 I     0 I  100.00%
                     +------+------+
  1.00        1    I  386 I     0 I    .00%
                     +------+------+
                        Overall  76.58%
```

---------------------- Variables in the Equation ----------------------

Variable	B	S.E.	Wald	df	Sig	R	Exp(B)
CHILDS	.1290	.0343	14.1230	1	.0002	.0822	1.1377
Constant	-1.4898	.1025	211.3728	1	.0000		

Figure 7.4 Logistic Regression Output

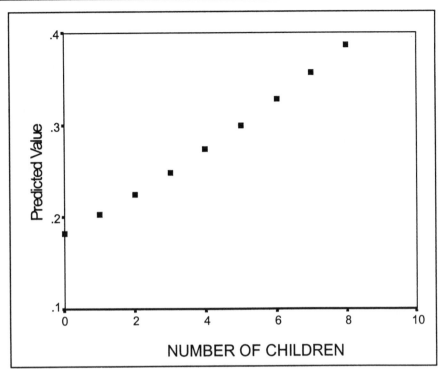

Figure 7.5 Graph of the Predicted Values of a Logistic Regression

From the graph represented in Figure 7.5, you can see that the relationship forms part of the steep section of the sigmoidal curve discussed above. There is a very strong relationship between the number of children and the likelihood of experiencing divorce or separation.

As with regression, it is possible to calculate a predicted value (in this case odds) for any value of the independent variable using the equation $\hat{G}=A+B(X)$.

$\hat{G}$ - The Predicted Log of the Odds
A - Constant
B - Logistic Regression Coefficient
X - The Given Value of the Independent Variable

In order to calculate the probability that a person with 4 children will have experienced divorce or separation, we first calculate the predicted log odds using the logistic regression equation.

$\hat{G} = A+B(X)$
$\hat{G} = -1.4898 + .1290(4)$
$\hat{G} = -1.4898 + .516$
$\hat{G} = -9738$

To convert Ĝ from log odds to natural odds, we would use the following equation:

$$odds = e^{\hat{G}}/1+e^{\hat{G}}$$
$$odds = e^{-.9738}/1+e^{-.9738}$$
$$odds = .3914/(1+.3914)$$
$$odds = .28$$

According to these calculations, there is a 28% probability that a person with 4 children will have experienced a divorce or separation.

It may seem like a lot of work to do these calculations. Remember that SPSS does these calculations for each of the cases in your data set when you save the predicted probabilities. You may find it useful in some circumstances to do these calculations using a scientific calculator, especially in setting parameters as part of interpreting multivariate logistic regression outcomes.

Multivariate Logistic Regression: An Example

In the above bivariate regression we found a relationship between the number of children and divorce and separation, but it runs counter to our hypothesis. Possibly age works as a spurious factor in producing this relationship. Because older people may be more likely to have experienced divorce or separation (simply as a product of living a longer time) and because older people will have had more time to have children, age may be working on these two factors simultaneously. The solution to solving this question is to engage in a multivariate logistic regression in order to control for the influence of age on divorce.

> *Statistics*
>> *Regression*
>>> *Logistic*
>>>> *Dependent*: DIVORCE2
>>>> *Covariates*: CHILDS
>>>>> AGE
>>> *Save*
>>>> *Predicted Values*: Probabilities

In analyzing the multivariate logistic regression (Figure 7.6), we find that the number of children in the family (CHILDS) is still significantly related to divorce (Sig=.0013). AGE (Sig=.3102) is not significantly related to divorce. We can conclude that age is not causing a spurious relationship between having children and experiencing divorce or separation.

Logistic Regression

```
        Total number of cases:       2904 (Unweighted)
     Number of selected cases:   2904
     Number of unselected cases: 0
     Number of selected cases:                 2904
     Number rejected because of missing data:  1258
     Number of cases included in the analysis: 1646
```

Dependent Variable Encoding:

```
Original       Internal
Value          Value
    .00        0
   1.00        1
```

Dependent Variable..   DIVORCE2   Divorce as Binomial

Beginning Block Number 0. Initial Log Likelihood Function

-2 Log Likelihood   1793.041

* Constant is included in the model.

Beginning Block Number 1. Method: Enter

Variable(s) Entered on Step Number
1..   CHILDS   NUMBER OF CHILDREN
         AGE   AGE OF RESPONDENT

Estimation terminated at iteration number 3 because
Log Likelihood decreased by less than .01 percent.

```
 -2 Log Likelihood       1778.148
 Goodness of Fit         1640.943
```

	Chi-Square	df	Significance
Model Chi-Square	14.893	2	.0006
Improvement	14.893	2	.0006

Classification Table for DIVORCE2

```
                       Predicted
                     .00    1.00     Percent Correct
                      0  I   1
Observed          +-------+-------+
    .00       0   I 1260 I    0 I   100.00%
                  +-------+-------+
   1.00       1   I  386 I    0 I     .00%
                  +-------+-------+
                     Overall  76.55%
```

-------------------- Variables in the Equation ----------------------

Variable	B	S.E.	Wald	df	Sig	R	Exp(B)
CHILDS	.1166	.0363	10.2967	1	.0013	.0680	1.1237
AGE	.0037	.0037	1.0298	1	.3102	.0000	1.0037
Constant	-1.6442	.1863	77.8614	1	.0000		

Figure 7.6 Multivariate Logistic Regression Output

It is possible to graph multivariate logistic regressions. Graphing logistic regressions with more than two independent variables can become quite involved. In most circumstances graphing either the bivariate relationship or trivariate relationships is sufficient for examining relationships in question. In fact, logistic regression is one of the operations which can use the three-dimensional scatter plot graphs to effectively display the complexities of relationships (Figure 7.7). To produce a three dimensional scatter plot of the above logistic regression, you will need to save the predicted probabilities. Remember these are new variables with the prefix PRE_. They will have a numeric indicator following the prefix and remember to use the most recently generated prediction. To graph the above regression, assuming your most recent prediction is PRE_2, you will perform the following operations:

Graph
> *Scatter*
>> *3-D*
>>> *Y Axis*: PRE_2
>>> *X Axis*: AGE
>>> *Z Axis*: CHILDS

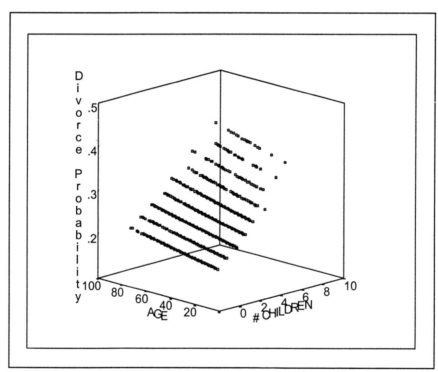

Figure 7.7 A Three Way Scatter Plot of a Logistic Regression Prediction

Calculating individual values is straightforward from the logistic regression output. The logistic regression equation is similar to that of the OLS regression equation. The log of the odds for the predicted value is produced by setting all of the parameters. For example, if we wanted to calculate the probability of a 30-year-old person with 2 children getting divorced, we would first calculate the predicted log of the odds.

$$\hat{G} = A + B_1(X_1) + B_2(X_2)$$
$$\hat{G} = -1.6442 + (.1166 * 2) + (.0037 * 30)$$
$$\hat{G} = -1.6442 + (.2332) + (.111)$$
$$\hat{G} = -1.3$$

To covert $\hat{G}$ from log odds to natural odds, we would use the following equation:

$$odds = e^{\hat{G}} / 1 + e^{\hat{G}}$$
$$odds = e^{-1.3} / 1 + e^{-1.13}$$
$$odds = .2725 / (1 + .2725)$$
$$odds = .2141$$

By performing these calculations, we determine that there is a 21% probability that a 30-year-old individual with 2 children has experienced a divorce or separation.

Summary
Logistic regression operates in ways similar to OLS regression. However, unlike OLS regression, logistic regression requires a dichotomous dependent variable and presents coefficients in terms of the log of the odds. By using the *recode* function of SPSS, it is possible to recode categorical and continuous variables to binary format. Logistic regression is often a viable alternative when the dependent variable does not conform to the expectations required for OLS regression.

Key Terms
Logistic Regression
Sigmoidal Curve
Binary Variable

References and Further Reading

Aldrich, John and Forrest Nelson. 1984. *Linear Probability, Logit and Probit Models*. Beverly Hills: Sage Publications.

Grimm, Laurence and Paul Yarnold. 1995. *Reading and Understanding Multivariate Statistics*. American Psychological Association: Washington D.C.

Hosmer, David and Stanley Lemeshow. 1989. *Applied Logistic Regression*. New York: John Wiley and Sons.

Chapter 7 Exercises

Name_____   Date_____

1. Using the GSS96 data and the computed variable DIVORCE2, examine whether the respondent's socioeconomic index score (SEI) has an effect on the likelihood of his/her having experienced a divorce or separation. Use logistic regression to generate the following information:

Constant   _____

Logistic Regression Coefficient SEI   _____

Significance   _____

Is this relationship statistically significant?   Yes   No

Do people scoring high on SEI have a
greater or lesser probability of
experiencing divorce or separation in
comparison to people scoring low on SEI?   Greater   Lesser   No Effect

2. Using the GSS96 data and the computed variable DIVORCE2, examine whether the respondent's education (EDUC) has an effect on the likelihood of his/her having experienced a divorce or separation. Use logistic regression to generate the following information:

Constant   _____

Logistic Regression Coefficient EDUC   _____

Significance   _____

Is this relationship statistically significant?   Yes   No

Do people with high levels of education
have a greater or lesser probability of
experiencing divorce or separation in
comparison to people with low education?   Greater   Lesser   No Effect

3. Recode a new binary variable indicating people's attitudes towards whether homosexuals should be allowed to teach using the variable COLHOMO. Name the new variable COLHOM2. Code those opposing homosexuals as teachers as 0 and those in favor as 1. Use the *Utilities-Variables* and *Frequencies* commands to facilitate your recoding of this variable. Supply the following information using *Frequencies* to check if your recode was successful.

COLHOMO	COLHOM2
count in favor _____	count coded 1_____
count opposed _____	count coded 0_____
count DK _____	count coded missing_____
count missing _____	

4. Using the GSS96 data and the computed variable COLHOM2, examine whether the respondent's education (EDUC) has an effect on the likelihood of his/her accepting homosexuals as teachers. Use logistic regression to generate the following information:

Constant   _____

Logistic Regression Coefficient EDUC   _____

Significance   _____

Is this relationship statistically significant?   Yes   No

Do people with higher educational attainment
have a greater or lesser probability of
supporting homosexuals as teachers
in comparison to people with low educations?   Greater   Lesser   No Effect

5. Using the output from the previous logistic regression, predict the odds of a person being in support of a homosexuals right to teach if the respondent has a high school education (12 years).

Step 1. Generate the log odds using the formula: $\hat{G} = A+B(X)$.   Log Odds_____

Step 2. Generate the odds using the formula: odds $= e^{\hat{G}}/1+e^{\hat{G}}$ Odds _____

6. Using the output from the previous logistic regression, predict the odds of a person being in support of a homosexuals right to teach if the respondent has a college education (16 years).

Step 1. Generate the log odds using the formula: $\hat{G} = A+B(X)$.   Log Odds_____

Step 2. Generate the odds using the formula: odds $= e^{\hat{G}}/1+e^{\hat{G}}$ Odds _____

7. Generate and print a scatter plot graph showing the predicted relationship between COLHOM2 and EDUC. Do your answers in questions 5 & 6 correspond with this graph?

Yes   No

8. Using the GSS96 data and the computed variable COLHOM2, examine whether the respondent's education (EDUC), controlling for the variable age (AGE), has an effect on the likelihood of his/her accepting homosexuals as teachers. Use logistic regression to generate the following information:

Constant   _____

Logistic Regression Coefficient EDUC   _____

Significance EDUC   _____

Is this relationship statistically significant?   Yes   No

Logistic Regression Coefficient AGE   _____

Significance AGE   _____

Is this relationship statistically significant?   Yes   No

Are older people more or less likely
to accept homosexuals as teachers in
comparison to younger people?   More   Less   No Effect

9.Using the output from the logistic regression, predict what the odds that a 65 year old person with 10 years of education will be in favor of homosexuals teaching.

Step 1. Generate the log of the odds using
the formula: $\hat{G} = A + B_1(X_1) + B_2(X_2)$ Log Odds_____

Step 2. Generate the odds using the formula: odds $= e^{\hat{G}}/1 + e^{\hat{G}}$ Odds _____

Chapter 8
Writing a Research Report

Overview

Writing the research report can be one of the most challenging parts of a research study. The main purpose of a research report is to condense the findings in order to enable the reader to understand the implications of the data analysis. This is not done by churning out lots of statistical output and leaving it for readers to decipher (frequently they will lack these skills). Rather, it is done by analyzing lots of statistical output, weeding out those analyses which are peripheral to the research question and keeping those analyses which are central to the study. Further, it involves reconfiguring those statistics into a format that is reader friendly, in the form of tables, graphs, and written text.

The structure of the research report may be influenced by a number of factors. For instance, in comparison to journal articles, evaluation reports will tend to have a more modest literature review but offer more weighty descriptions of the particular program being assessed. The reason for this variation is that different types of readers often have very different needs. Different readers also have different capacities to understand the statistical content of our studies. A research report written to a general audience will have a decidedly different content than a report written to a professional audience. Tailoring the report to coincide with the readers' needs and their statistical capabilities is a guiding principle that underpins the writing of the research report.

We will be using the journal article format as a guide to writing the research report. This structure, of course, can be modified depending on your (and the readers') needs. Journal articles tend to be divided into eight sections:

Title
Abstract
Introduction
Literature review
Methods
Findings
Conclusion
References

We will be examining each section in turn, the purpose of each section, and the ways in which statistics and text are used to relate our understandings of the social world.

The Title

Report titles offer a concise description of the research report. The title can make or break an article because it is what is likely to attract a reader to the report. If a title lacks the necessary content, or presents the subject in a less than satisfactory manner, it may discourage potential readers from examining the report. The minimal standard for a title is that it be short (5-10 words) and that it offer some information about the research topic.

It is not in a researcher's interest to pick the types of titles that appear in *Cosmopolitan* or *People* magazine. Consider the merits of these titles:

"Who Will Save the Children?"

"Adversity Against All Odds"

"Desperate, But Not Defeated!"

While these titles are catchy, they share in common two essential problems. The first problem is that they do not give sufficient information to enable the reader to get an immediate grasp of the issue being addressed in the report. The reader does not know what is threatening children, what is the adversity against the odds, or who is desperate but not defeated. The second concern is that these titles imply that the researcher is an advocate of a political cause, rather than an objective analyst of data. Some researchers question the notion of objectivity in social science research (e.g., Reinharz 1979) and assert that all studies have varying levels of researcher bias. I am in much agreement with these concerns. However, the convention in scientific writing is to engage in rhetoric which appears as objective and neutral as possible. Because our reports are generally written to the scientific community, or to people who trust our attempts at objectivity, it is to the writers' advantage to write in a non-inflammatory style.

Here are a few more titles, drawn from the American Sociological Review:

"The Democratic Class Struggle in the United States, 1948-1992"

"The Impact of Reagan's New Federalism on Business Failures"

"Organizational Mortality in Peace Movement Organizations."

I suspect these titles strike you as being less "catchy," but I suggest they are much better than the previous titles. Note how each title offers substantial information about the topic the research article is addressing. Also note that the topic is given in a manner which is implies that the study will offer a balanced evaluation of the data. For example, while it is possible that Reagan's new federalism increased business failures, the title also makes clear that it is possible that the opposite may have occurred.

The Abstract

Although the abstract is the first major section of a research report, it is usually the section which is written the last. The reason for this is that the abstract is the product of distilling the report into a concise summary. The length of the abstract can vary, but it should be under 150 words (approximately half a page of double space text). It serves very much like an "executive summary" in business reports. The abstract should contain information about the research question, data, findings, and conclusions of the study. The trick in an abstract is to use words as effectively as possible because space is very limited.

Figure 8.1 A Sample Abstract

<u>Everyday Forms of Employee Resistance</u>

Drawing on empirical material collected from over 250 individuals employed in a variety of short-term positions, this article examines how temporary employees pursue grievances against their employing organizations. The findings indicate that temporary employees generally respond to offensive behavior on the part of their employers in nonaggressive ways. Gossip, toleration, and resignation are popular, while occasionally grievances are expressed by theft, sabotage, or noncooperation. Collective responses, formal complaints, and legal action are rare. These restrained responses are traced not to the severity of injustices but to the social environment associated with temporary employment, where workers are loosely tied to their organizations and one another. This research may help explain the decline of organized resistance in the contemporary workplace.

Source: Tucker, James. 1993. "Everyday Forms of Employee Resistance."
        Sociological Forum 8:25-45.

The above example is a good illustration of a well written abstract. There are a few things in the abstract which deserve note. The author starts the abstract by immediately discussing the research question and the data. The author then discusses the findings and briefly explains the relationships (in order of magnitude) without using any statistics. The author then concludes with a brief statement about the relevance of this research to our understandings of social relationships.

Again, I would not suggest writing the abstract before writing all of the other sections of the research report. Once the rest of the report is written, you will probably find that this section will fall into place quite readily.

The Introduction

The introduction invites the reader to examine the rest of the report. In this section the writer "sells" the report to readers, informing them of the research question and why this question is important. This section can usually be quite short (1-3 double spaced typed pages) and the length will depend on the type of research question addressed.

After reading through the introduction, the reader should have a very clear idea of the question the writer is addressing. Good introductions will often include the phrase "In this paper I...." This brief phrase forces the writer to come to terms with the specific purpose of the paper and to focus the rest of the report accordingly.

In writing the introduction, global and unsupported statements should be avoided. Consider this introductory sentence: "The growth in teenage births is a huge social problem." While this may seem intuitively appealing, the statement is factually incorrect because teenage births have declined rather than increased over the past 24 years. This introduction could be improved significantly by providing factual information, such as "According to the Bureau of the Census, the teenage birth rate has declined from 69.5/1000 teenage women in 1970 to 59.9/1000 in 1994." The introduction then can build a compelling argument why it is still important to study teenage births in the context of current demographic trends.

Generally, the introduction should not serve as the conclusion of the study. Consider this introductory sentence: "In this paper I will prove that teenagers get pregnant because they lack solid moral values." It is important to remember that scientific methodology cannot prove anything, it can only find support for some hypotheses and refute other hypotheses. It would be a considerable improvement to rephrase this sentence as: "In this paper I will examine the degree to which personal values influence teenagers' risks for pregnancy." The introduction is designed only to open the research question.

The Literature Review

Because this book has emphasized data analysis, I have thus far not given sufficient attention to the literature review component of social science research. The sociologist Max Weber (1946) argued that science is a cumulative endeavor and that all of our work as scientists rests on the shoulders of scientists who preceded us. The literature review is aimed at simultaneously acknowledging other researchers' contributions to our knowledge while also informing the reader of how these contributions relate to our research question. The literature review is an appraisal of what is known and what is not known about the research question being addressed. Depending on the scope of the research project, typical literature reviews in journal articles range from 4-10 pages of double spaced type.

At a bare minimum, a literature review is an overview of the essential findings from a list of articles which address issues related to the research question. However, a literature review can be significantly improved by providing some structure which links these articles together. For example, in a study of factors associated with family violence, I organized the literature review by first talking about studies which looked at gender and family violence, then age and family violence, then race/ethnicity and family violence, then socioeconomic status and family violence. Providing a structure such as this enables the reader to get a solid understanding of the current knowledge about these relationships (see Straus and Sweet 1992).

This strategy is not the only way to provide a structure to a literature review. In some circumstances it may be more useful to link studies together because of similarities in methodologies. For example, a study on behaviors of the poor could link the studies by first discussing the findings of participant-observation studies, then the findings of cross sectional survey studies, and then findings based on panel design studies. Each methodology will reveal different aspects of the behaviors of concern. In rare circumstances, it might even be appropriate to organize a literature review by the dates of the studies: for example, comparing studies on television viewing behavior performed in the 1950s with studies examining television viewing behavior in the 1990s. There are other strategies of providing a structure as well. By far, though, the weakest literature review discusses studies in random order.

The Methods

As with every other section of the report, the methodology section should be written in as concise a manner as possible. In this section, the concern is to explain the data collection methods, sampling strategies, sample sizes, indicators, and any reworking of the data in the study. The length of the methodology section will vary, depending on the complexities involved in the data collection and analysis procedures, but generally this section can be written in 2-5 double spaced typed pages. Examining the methodology sections from journal articles is a good way to learn how this information is typically provided.

While writing the methodology section, it is useful to take the perspective of the intelligent skeptical reader. This reader will be looking for weaknesses and flaws in the study and will be inclined to distrust conclusions unless given reasons to bolster confidence in the study findings. With this in mind, the intelligent skeptical reader will ask questions such as:

Are the data suited to the research question?

Is the sample size large enough?

Is the sample a representative sample?

Is the sample appropriate to the study?

Are the indicators reliable and valid?

Does the researcher measure factors which could cause spurious findings?

Does the researcher use analytic techniques suited to the data?

With each of these questions, the reader is asking "Why should I trust what the researcher is later going to be telling me about social behavior?" The methodology section builds that trust by carefully laying out the empirical basis of the study.

The methodology section should, at a minimum, address the following information:

The methods of data collection.

The sample size.

Modifications made to the data.

The types of statistical procedures used.

The Findings

The findings section details all of the results of the study. While the researchers may have found many interesting results, the concern here is to focus the discussion only on those results which directly relate to the research question posed in the introduction. It is in this section that graphs and tables are presented showing the relationships of interest. These relationships are also described using text. Depending on the complexities of the study, this section typically ranges from 6-12 double spaced typed pages.

There is an old maxim that social scientists read tables and ignore the text and "regular people" read the text and ignore the tables. There is considerable truth to this statement and the findings section should be written accordingly. Tables and graphs should be rich with statistical information relating to the research question. The text serves the purpose of translating these statistics into a form which "regular people" can understand. This involves describing the relationships in a manner which largely avoids the use of numerical descriptors. Tables may show percentages or regression coefficients, but the text accompanying the tables should be phrased in terms of "positive" and "negative" relationships.

One of the best ways to organize the findings section is to address results in relation to hypotheses. Your study should come to some conclusion in relation to each testable proposition posed in the introduction and literature review. With some thought, you may be able to construct a table which can effectively display all of the information needed, including significance tests, sample sizes, etc.

Figure 8.1 illustrates how a well-constructed table improves raw SPSS output. One of the chief advantages is that the table effectively conveys a lot of information in a concise manner. The reader is supplied with the logistic regression coefficients, standard errors, the constant, and significance tests for two different regressions. In academic journals it is common to observe the results of many regressions presented in a single table.

Figure 8.2 A Sample Table

TABLE 1. LOGISTIC REGRESSION OF VERBAL/SYMBOLIC AGGRESSION

| | Verbal/Symbolic Aggression | | | |
| | Man-to-Woman | | Woman-to-Man | |
Independent Variable	Coefficient	SE	Coefficient	SE
Gender	0.20**	.077	0.39**	.077
Age	-0.02**	.003	-0.02**	.003
Number of children	-0.09**	.033	-0.05	.030
Drunk	0.01**	.003	0.04**	.009
High on drugs	0.00	.001	0.01**	.002
Physical aggression	1.35**	.082	1.30**	.074
Couple conflict	0.93**	.052	0.83**	.050
Logit Constant	-1.82**	.162	-1.66**	.163

*p<.05   **p<.01

Source: Straus, Murray and Stephen Sweet. 1992. "Verbal/Symbolic Aggression in Couples." Journal of Marriage and the Family 54:346-357.

The Conclusion

The conclusion provides an overview of the findings in relation to the research question posed in the introduction. The intent of the conclusion is to bridge the study findings out to that of the social world by **generalizing** the findings. To generalize findings is to relate the findings to social behavior outside of the study, or to behavior that is commonly observed in society. The conclusion also serves to reinforce the theoretical or practical implications of the study findings.

The process of generalizing the findings to the external social world requires consideration of **external validity**. External validity refers to the degree to which the study findings accurately describe social behavior outside of the confines of the study. In order to assess external validity, the researcher should consider the limitations of the study. For example, laboratory experiments on human subjects are often suspect of external validity because they place people in contrived situations (Campbell and Stanley 1963). A biased sample could also be a threat to external validity. If a sample consists only of college freshman, for example, the researcher should be cautious in generalizing the findings to the general population. As a researcher, it is unlikely that you will know all the potential sources of external invalidity as you generalize findings. It is your obligation, however, to discuss the potential limitations of your study in the conclusion of your research report.

One positive way to conclude a research report is to acknowledge the limitations of the study and to open the topic to further related questions. The researcher can state "In this study I showed..." and then go on to say "Further research needs to be done to find out if...." Science is a never ending process and a strong conclusion acknowledges this facet of our collective endeavor.

References

The reference section provides a list of sources referred to in the report. Each discipline specifies different formats for referencing sources. It is important in the reference, no matter what the chosen format, to provide sufficient information so that any interested reader can locate that original source of information.

The following are some examples of how the American Sociological Association suggests referencing books, articles and government documents.

Figure 8.3 ASA Reference Examples

<u>Books</u>
>Berlin, Gorden and Andrew Sum. 1988. *Toward a More Perfect Union: Basic Skills, Poor Families, and Our Economic Future.* New York: Ford Foundation.

<u>Articles from Collected Works</u>
>Clausen, John A. 1972. "The Life Course of Individuals." Pp. 457-514 in *Aging and Society*, vol. 3, *A Sociology of Age Stratification*, edited by M.W. Riley, M. Johnson, and A. Foner. New York: Russell Sage.

<u>Articles in Journals</u>
>Goodman, Leo A. 1947. "The Analysis of Systems of Qualitative Variables When Some of the Variables Are Unobservable. Part 1 - A Modified Latent Structure Approach." *American Journal of Sociology* 79:1179-259.

<u>Articles from Newspapers and Magazines</u>
>Guiles, Melinda and Krystal Miller. 1990. "Mazda and Mitsubishi-Chrysler Venture Cut Output, Following Big Three's Lead." *Wall Street Journal*, January 12, pp. A2, A12.

<u>Government Documents</u>
>U.S. Bureau of the Census. 1960. *Characteristics of Population.* Vol 1. Washington, DC: U.S. Government Printing Office.

>Source: American Sociological Association. 1996. *American Sociological Association Style Guide.* Washington, DC: American Sociological Association.

Summary

SPSS can generate a great variety of statistical output. It is the researcher's challenge to make the statistical analysis understood by others interested in their research questions. The research report is essential in conveying this information. A well-written report is concise (usually under 20 double spaced pages in length). It conveys statistical information in numeric form and describes relationships with prose. All good reports explain the relevance of the study, as well as potential limitations.

Key Terms
Abstract
External Validity
Generalization

References and Further Reading
American Psychological Association. 1995. *Publication Manual of the American Psychological Association.* 4th ed. Washington, DC: American Psychological Association.

American Sociological Association. 1996. *American Sociological Association Style Guide.* Washington, DC: American Sociological Association.

Becker, Howard. 1984. *Writing for the Social Sciences.* Chicago, IL: University of Chicago Press.

Campbell, Donald and Julian Stanley. 1963. *Experimental and Quasi-Experimental Designs for Research.* Chicago: Rand McNally.

Reinharz, Shulamit. 1979. *On Becoming a Social Scientist.* San Francisco: Jossey-Bass Publishers.

Straus, Murray and Stephen Sweet. 1992. "Verbal/Symbolic Aggression in Couples: Incidence Rates and Relationships to Personal Characteristics." *Journal of Marriage and the Family* 54:346-357.

Tucker, James. 1993. Everyday Forms of Employee Resistance." *Sociological Forum* 8:25-45.

Weber, Max. 1946. *From Max Weber: Essays in Sociology.* London: Routledge & Kegan Paul.

Chapter 9
Research Projects

Overview

This chapter outlines some potential research projects which can be tackled using SPSS and the data sets provided with this book. It also discusses some potential sources for publically available data suited to other research projects and the advantages of secondary data analysis.

Secondary Data Analysis

This chapter concludes with some ideas for research projects which can begin with data included with this text. Before I outline some of these projects, it is important to recognize the relative advantages and disadvantages of engaging in secondary data analysis. **Secondary data analysis** occurs when a researcher takes advantage of information already compiled by other researchers. When researchers can use existing data they can be thankful because collecting and compiling data is one of the most time consuming steps in the research process. If data are already available which relate to a research question, it can often times shave years and thousands of dollars off a research project.

This being said, secondary data also impose limitations and logistical problems onto many research projects. One problem is that sometimes these data sets come with less than complete documentation on how the data were collected and compiled. Unless the primary data analyst was considerate enough to keep careful track of all changes made to the data and document these changes, the secondary analyst may have difficulty discerning what each variable represents. Suppose, for instance, that a data set has a variable indicating a "racism tendency." If we do not know how these data were computed, we are limited in understanding exactly what this variable actually represents. Also, if the data set does not include information on how the data were initially compiled (e.g., phone

157

interviews or face-to-face interviews), we lose much of our capacity to evaluate the quality of those data. Thankfully researchers are becoming more and more sensitive to the needs of secondary analysts and are keeping detailed records of their methodology.

Another concern is that sometimes data may be structured in a manner which is not immediately conducive to the analytic procedures that the secondary analyst wants to perform. Reconfiguring the data can sometimes be a considerable technological challenge. For instance, in compiling the STATES.SAV data (these are secondary data), I ultimately had to invert the entire table so that the rows became the columns and the columns became the rows. I also had to merge a number of files together and generate labels. SPSS has the capability of performing tasks such as this, but it ultimately took a bit of trial and error to get the data restructured to the form on your disk.

A third consideration is that secondary analysis often imposes a research question on data which may not have been intended for that purpose. For instance, banking records, such as mortgage approvals, are kept for bookkeeping practices and are generally not kept for social scientists. If we were to look for evidence of racism in mortgage approval practices, we would want information on each applicant's race. Possibly this information is lacking because it was not a major concern for the initial record keeper. In a circumstance such as this, the secondary data analyst may be able to add other information to the data set which can contribute to the research question. For instance, mortgage information may lack the variable "race" but it will contain information on the applicant's address. The researcher can then look to see if applicants living in predominantly black neighborhoods are turned down for mortgages in comparison to applicants living in primarily white neighborhoods. This, of course, requires gathering more data which must be integrated with the data set. The secondary data analyst must take into account the limitations of any set of data. In some circumstances all of the necessary information will be available. I suspect, however, that the majority of projects relying on secondary data analysis force researchers to accept the limitations of the data obtained and use creativity to minimize these limitations.

Publically Available Data

There are a number of organizations which provide publically available data. These data can be used for secondary data analysis by individual researchers, but generally cannot be redistributed without the permission of the organization that possesses these data. Currently the American Sociological Association lists a number of these resources and periodically updates a web page which describes the content of these data sets and how to obtain the data. You may find it of value to examine the American Sociological Association web page to learn of some of the many opportunities to examine secondary data.

American Sociological Association
http://www.asanet.org/

The American Sociological Association's web site, as of this writing, lists 27 organizations and research projects which are making their data available for public use. These include:

General Social Survey.

International Social Survey Program.

The Wisconsin Longitudinal Study.

The National Survey of Families and Households.

The Panel Study of Income Dynamics.

Health Retirement Study and Survey of Asset and
Health Dynamics Among the Oldest Old.

The National Longitudinal Study of Adolescent Health.

Children of the National Longitudinal Survey of Youth.

Mexican Migration Project.

Inter-University Consortium for Political and Social Research.

Sociometrics Data Archives.

Manpower Demonstration Research Corporation.

Consortium for International Earth Science Information Network.

JSTOR (Journal Storage).

National Archives.

U.S. Department of Education--National Center for
Education Statistics.

U.S. Department of Justice--Bureau of Justice Statistics.

U.S. Department of Labor--Bureau of Labor Statistics,
National Longitudinal Surveys.

National Institute on Aging--Demography and Population
Epidemiology Branch.

National Institute of Child Health and Human
Development-Demographic and Behavioral Sciences Branch.

Centers for Disease Control and Prevention--National Center
for Health Statistics, Data Dissemination Branch.

Centers for Disease Control and Prevention--National Center
for Health Statistics, Division of Vital Statistics, Mortality
Statistics Branch.

Centers for Disease Control and Prevention--National Center
for Health Statistics, Natality, Marriage, and Divorce Statistics
Branch.

Centers for Disease Control and Prevention--National Center
for Health Statistics, National Hospital Discharge Survey.

Centers for Disease Control and Prevention--National Center
for Health Statistics, The National Health Interview Survey.

Centers for Disease Control and Prevention--Center for Chronic
Disease Prevention and Health Promotion, Behavioral Risk Factor
Surveillance System.

Council of Professional Associations on Federal Statistics.

The American Sociological Association describes these organizations and research projects, as well as how to contact the distributors of these data. In some circumstances these data are ready to analyze. In other circumstances you will need to merge or reconfigure files to suit your needs.

Potential Research Projects
In the following pages I will describe some potential research projects which can be tackled with the data included with this book. Before embarking on these projects, I think it may be wise to review some of the central lessons forwarded in this book in order to guide your approach.

Research projects are guided by developing research questions and using data which fits a research question. In the potential research projects, I will suggest a general research topic and loosely defined research questions. You will need to make a clear research question and evaluate the degree to which the data are suited to answering this question. One of the first tasks you will need to perform is locating variables which relate to that research question. This includes finding relevant independent and dependent variables and assessing the degree to which these variables are accurate indicators of the concepts you want to examine.

It is to the researcher's advantage to understand what is already known about a research question. Therefore you will find it useful to engage in a literature review on the subject. The depth of this literature review can be of your (or possibly your instructor's) discretion. However, you should have a reasonable understanding of what to anticipate in the data analysis based on previous research in this area.

Empirical studies are hypothesis driven. Once you have developed an understanding of the relationships previously revealed by other researchers, you should be able to develop clearly framed hypotheses concerning the relationships between each independent and dependent variable. These hypotheses should be embedded in a larger theoretical understanding of the basis of social behavior and social experience.

Analysis of the data occurs in three stages. The first stage is univariate analysis, where the researcher examines the structure, central tendency, and spread of individual variables. The second stage is bivariate analysis, where the researcher examines the relationships between two variables in isolation from other variables. The third stage is multivariate analysis, where multiple variables are examined in conjunction with one another in order to control for extraneous factors and examine cumulative effects.

Once you have gained an understanding of the nuances revealed through the data analysis, the research report is written. The report distills the analysis to the most essential information so that readers can understand the relationships revealed in the data analysis. The report will contain carefully constructed tables and graphs which yield maximum content in minimal space. It also includes written descriptions of the relationships revealed.

The report will conclude with a summary of hypotheses supported and not supported. In some circumstances you will likely find that the data do not support the hypothesis constructed. In some of these cases, you may conclude that the relationship is nonexistent. However, it is also important at this stage of the study to critically evaluate the limitations of the data. State level data, for instance, covers very large geographic regions. Therefore in some circumstances the data may gloss over important variations within each state. For example, I am writing this book in St. Lawrence County, a very isolated and rural part of New York state. Our experiences in St. Lawrence County are very different than that of residents of Brooklyn County in New York City. However, because New York state (not the individual counties) is our unit of analysis in the STATES.SAV data, the variation between counties cannot be examined. In some circumstances, lumping of social experience into such a large geographic area may limit the validity of the measures. This may be one consideration (among others) that you may wish to consider in evaluating the degree to which a theory is ultimately maintained or rejected. The research report should conclude with an analysis of these limitations, as well as with some suggestions for future research.

Key Terms
Secondary Data Analysis
Publically Available Data

Research Project 1: Racism

Social theory posits that people sometimes have prejudicial thoughts, which in turn lead them to discriminate against members of particular racial groups in society. This constitutes overt discrimination. Social theory also posits that there are structural factors which limit the opportunities of group members. Social structure includes the ways in which schools are funded, jobs distributed, infrastructure maintained, etc.. If a racial group resides in an area which is deprived, they become deprived as a result. Can you determine, based on the GSS96.SAV data and the STATE.SAV data, the degree to which prejudice, overt discrimination, and structural discrimination against African Americans persists in the United States?

Suggestions for Data Analysis:

A. Make a list of variables from the STATES.SAV data and the GSS96.SAV data which relate to this research question.

B. Determine which variables are independent variables and which variables are dependent variables.

C. Examine the structure of each of these variables to determine if they are continuous or categorical variables.

D. Develop a clear hypothesis how each independent variable will be related to the dependent variable.

E. Perform Univariate Analysis
   Means, Medians, Modes, Standard Deviations, Stem and Leaf Plots, Box Plots, Histograms, Pie Charts, Bar Charts.

F. Perform Bivariate Analysis
   Crosstabulations, Comparison of Means, Correlations, Significance Tests, Box Plots, Bar Charts, Scatter Plots.

G. Perform Multivariate Analysis
   OLS Regression, Logistic Regression, Significance Tests, Scatter Plots.

Research Project 2: Suicide

What explains why a person choses to terminate his or her own life? On the one hand, this can possibly be attributed to psychological factors, such as depression. On the other hand, it can be caused by social forces such as living in a society which is characterized as socially disorganized (e.g., lots of crime, unemployment, etc.). Can you determine the degree to which social psychological factors influence a person's willingness to accept suicide as a viable alternative to life's problems using the GSS96.SAV data? Can you then determine the degree to which social structural factors influence variation in suicide rates using the STATE.SAV data?

Suggestions for Data Analysis:

A.   Make a list of variables from the STATES.SAV data and the GSS96.SAV data which relate to this research question.

B.   Determine which variables are independent variables and which variables are dependent variables.

C.   Examine the structure of each of these variables to determine if they are continuous or categorical variables.

D.   Develop a clear hypothesis how each independent variable will be related to the dependent variable.

E.   Perform Univariate Analysis
         Means, Medians, Modes, Standard Deviations, Stem and Leaf Plots, Box Plots, Histograms, Pie Charts, Bar Charts.

F.   Perform Bivariate Analysis
         Crosstabulations, Comparison of Means, Correlations, Significance Tests, Box Plots, Bar Charts, Scatter Plots.

G.   Perform Multivariate Analysis
         OLS Regression, Logistic Regression, Significance Tests, Scatter Plots.

Research Project 3: Politics

Politicians are often interested in targeting specific groups of people because they know that individuals vary in their attitudes and likelihood of participating in the political process. What factors contribute to the variation in political participation? One set of factors may be social structural factors, such as the degree to which citizens are taxed or impacted by industrial waste. Using the STATES.SAV data determine the degree to which structural factors influence political participation. People are also likely to vary in their political involvement due to social psychological factors. Using the GSS96.SAV data, examine the social psychological factors which influence political involvement and political orientation.

Suggestions for Data Analysis:

A.   Make a list of variables from the STATES.SAV data and the GSS96.SAV data which relate to this research question.

B.   Determine which variables are independent variables and which variables are dependent variables.

C.   Examine the structure of each of these variables to determine if they are continuous or categorical variables.

D.   Develop a clear hypothesis how each independent variable will be related to the dependent variable.

E.   Perform Univariate Analysis
        Means, Medians, Modes, Standard Deviations, Stem and Leaf Plots, Box Plots, Histograms, Pie Charts, Bar Charts.

F.   Perform Bivariate Analysis
        Crosstabulations, Comparison of Means, Correlations, Significance Tests, Box Plots, Bar Charts, Scatter Plots.

G.   Perform Multivariate Analysis
        OLS Regression, Logistic Regression, Significance Tests, Scatter Plots.

Research Project 4: Criminality

Some places have high crime rates and other places have low crime rates. What social factors contribute to this variation of crime from place to place? Do the methods of treating/punishing criminals have an effect on deterring crime? Use the STATES.SAV data to examine these issues. Pay particular attention to variation between types of crime in your analysis.

Suggestions for Data Analysis:

A.   Make a list of variables from the STATES.SAV data and the data which relate to this research question.

B.   Determine which variables are independent variables and which variables are dependent variables.

C.   Examine the structure of each of these variables to determine if they are continuous or categorical variables.

D.   Develop a clear hypothesis how each independent variable will be related to the dependent variable.

E.   Perform Univariate Analysis
        Means, Medians, Modes, Standard Deviations, Stem and Leaf Plots, Box Plots, Histograms, Pie Charts, Bar Charts.

F.   Perform Bivariate Analysis
        Crosstabulations, Comparison of Means, Correlations, Significance Tests, Box Plots, Bar Charts, Scatter Plots.

G.   Perform Multivariate Analysis
        OLS Regression, Logistic Regression, Significance Tests, Scatter Plots.

Research Project 5: Welfare

There is considerable variation in welfare use. One cause for this variation may be that individuals have different expectations of what they are entitled to receive just by living in our society. On the other hand, there may be social structural factors (e.g., unemployment) which either force or lure individuals to use welfare as a means of survival. Use the GSS96.SAV data to examine variation in peoples attitudes toward entitlement programs. Use the STATE.SAV data to examine which structural factors influence welfare consumption.

Suggestions for Data Analysis:

A.   Make a list of variables from the STATES.SAV data and the GSS96.SAV data which relate to this research question.

B.   Determine which variables are independent variables and which variables are dependent variables.

C.   Examine the structure of each of these variables to determine if they are continuous or categorical variables.

D.   Develop a clear hypothesis how each independent variable will be related to the dependent variable.

E.   Perform Univariate Analysis
        Means, Medians, Modes, Standard Deviations, Stem and Leaf Plots, Box Plots, Histograms, Pie Charts, Bar Charts.

F.   Perform Bivariate Analysis
        Crosstabulations, Comparison of Means, Correlations, Significance Tests, Box Plots, Bar Charts, Scatter Plots.

G.   Perform Multivariate Analysis
        OLS Regression, Logistic Regression, Significance Tests, Scatter Plots.

Research Project 6: Sexual Behavior

There is considerable variation in sexual behavior on an individual level, as well as by geographic locale. Using the GSS96.SAV data, determine the social psychological factors which contribute to a permissive attitude toward sexual freedom. Using the STATES.SAV data, examine the variation in birth rates to identify social structural factors which also potentially contribute to permissive sexual lifestyles.

Suggestions for Data Analysis:

A.   Make a list of variables from the STATES.SAV data and the GSS96.SAV data which relate to this research question.

B.   Determine which variables are independent variables and which variables are dependent variables.

C.   Examine the structure of each of these variables to determine if they are continuous or categorical variables.

D.   Develop a clear hypothesis how each independent variable will be related to the dependent variable.

E.   Perform Univariate Analysis
          Means, Medians, Modes, Standard Deviations, Stem and Leaf Plots, Box Plots, Histograms, Pie Charts, Bar Charts.

F.   Perform Bivariate Analysis
          Crosstabulations, Comparison of Means, Correlations, Significance Tests, Box Plots, Bar Charts, Scatter Plots.

G.   Perform Multivariate Analysis
          OLS Regression, Logistic Regression, Significance Tests, Scatter Plots.

Research Project 7: Education

Individuals' educational attainment can be influenced by their personal background and the type of society they live in. Using the GSS96.SAV data, examine the degree to which educational attainment varies by a person's biographical background. Then using the STATES.SAV data, examine the degree to which social structural factors influence educational attainment across the United States.

Suggestions for Data Analysis:

A.   Make a list of variables from the STATES.SAV data and the GSS96.SAV data which relate to this research question.

B.   Determine which variables are independent variables and which variables are dependent variables.

C.   Examine the structure of each of these variables to determine if they are continuous or categorical variables.

D.   Develop a clear hypothesis how each independent variable will be related to the dependent variable.

E.   Perform Univariate Analysis
Means, Medians, Modes, Standard Deviations, Stem and Leaf Plots, Box Plots, Histograms, Pie Charts, Bar Charts.

F.   Perform Bivariate Analysis
Crosstabulations, Comparison of Means, Correlations, Significance Tests, Box Plots, Bar Charts, Scatter Plots.

G.   Perform Multivariate Analysis
OLS Regression, Logistic Regression, Significance Tests, Scatter Plots.

Research Project 8: Your Topic

There are many other variables included in the STATES.SAV data set and the GSS96.SAV data set. Can you develop a research question which uses these data to their fullest potential? Ultimately you may need to search for additional data to merge with the STATE.SAV data, but don't let this stop you. That is to be expected in social research.

Suggestions for Data Analysis:

A.   Make a list of variables from the STATES.SAV data and the GSS96.SAV data which relate to this research question.

B.   Determine which variables are independent variables and which variables are dependent variables.

C.   Examine the structure of each of these variables to determine if they are continuous or categorical variables.

D.   Develop a clear hypothesis how each independent variable will be related to the dependent variable.

E.   Perform Univariate Analysis
        Means, Medians, Modes, Standard Deviations, Stem and Leaf Plots, Box Plots, Histograms, Pie Charts, Bar Charts.

F.   Perform Bivariate Analysis
        Crosstabulations, Comparison of Means, Correlations, Significance Tests, Box Plots, Bar Charts, Scatter Plots.

G.   Perform Multivariate Analysis
        OLS Regression, Logistic Regression, Significance Tests, Scatter Plots.

APPENDIX 1: STATES.SAV DESCRIPTIVES

Descriptive Statistics

		N	Mean
CJC199	'Juvenile Arrest Rate 1995'	47	10052.6
CJC202	'Juvenile Arrest Rate:Crime Index Offenses 1995'	47	3268.29
CJC205	'Juvenile Arrest Rate:Violent Crime 1995'	47	455.0702
CJC208	'Juvenile Arrest Rate:Murder 1995'	47	10.7511
CJC211	'Juvenile Arrest Rate:Rape 1995'	47	19.0447
CJC214	'Juvenile Arrest Rate:Robbery 1995'	47	156.5638
CJC217	'Juvenile Arrest Rate:Aggravated Assault 1995'	47	268.7064
CJC220	'Juvenile Arrest Rate:Property Crime 1995'	47	2813.23
CJC223	'Juvenile Arrest Rate:Burglary 1995'	47	425.1340
CJC226	'Arrest Rate of Juveniles:Larceny&Theft 1995'	47	2040.76
CJC229	'Arrest Rate of Juveniles:Motor Vehicle Theft 1995'	47	307.0340
CJC232	'Juvenile Arrest Rate:Arson 1995'	47	40.3170
CJC235	'Arrest Rate of Juveniles:Weapons Violations 1995'	47	187.9957
CJC238	'Juvenile Arrest Rate:Driving Under the Influence 1995'	47	57.0383
CJC241	'Arrest Rate of Juveniles:Drug Abuse Violations 1995'	47	637.8809
CJC244	'Arrest Rate of Juveniles:Sex Offenses 1995'	47	54.2362
CJC247	'Juvenile Arrest Rate:Prostitution&Commercial Vice 1995'	47	3.8872
CJC250	'Juvenile Arrest Rate:Offenses Against Families&Children 1995'	47	34.2723
CJC253	'Rate of Child Abuse&Neglect 1994'	48	1617.23
CJC255	'Juvenile Custody Rate:1991'	51	241.0196
CJC256	'Juvenile Custody Rate:Public Facilities 1991'	51	183.5294
CJC257	'Juvenile Custody Rate:Private Facilities 1991'	51	57.4902
CPC100	'AIDS-Related Death Rate of State Prisoners 1994'	48	62.8125
CPC101	'Deaths of State Prisoners by AIDS as%of All Prison Deaths 1994'	48	18.0292
CPC102	'State Prisoners Known HIV Positive HIV Infection AIDS 1994'	48	453.1042
CPC103	'State Prisoners Known HIV Positive AIDS as%of Prison Pop 94'	48	1.5708
CPC104	'Deaths of State Prisoners by Suicide 1994'	47	3.2979
CPC105	'Deaths of State Prisoners by Suicide as%of All Prison Deaths 1994'	47	8.6989
CPC106	'Adults Under State Correctional Supervision 1993'	51	92388.3
CPC107	'% of Population Under State Correctional Supervision 1993'	51	2.1765
CPC112	'State&Loc Gvt Employees in Corrections 1994'	51	11459.4
CPC113	'State&Loc Gvt Employees in Corrections as%of State&LocGvt 94'	51	3.6694
CPC122	'Jail&Detention Centers 1993'	46	71.8261
CPC137	'Alcohol&Drug Treatment Units 1994'	50	165.4200
CPC138	'Alcohol&Drug Treatment Admits 1994'	50	36136.6
CPC139	'Male Admits to Alcohol&Drug Treat Programs 1994'	50	24767.0
CPC140	'Male Admits to Alcohol&Drug Treat Programs as%of All Admits 94'	50	71.1636
CPC141	'Female Admits to Alcohol&Drug Treat Programs 1994'	50	9846.60
CPC142	'Female Admits to Alcohol&Drug Treat Programs as%of All Admits 94'	50	27.2484

171

Descriptive Statistics

	N	Mean
CPC143 'White Admits to Alcohol&Drug Treat Programs 1994'	50	20462.4
CPC144 'White Admits to Alcohol&Drug Treat Programs as%of All Admits 94'	50	62.4026
CPC145 'Black Admits to Alcohol&Drug Treat Programs 1994'	50	9341.24
CPC146 'Black Admits to Alcohol&Drug Treat Programs as%of All Admits 94'	50	22.2100
CPC147 'Hisp Admits to Alcohol&Drug Treat Programs 1994'	38	3739.05
CPC148 'Hisp Admits to Alcohol&Drug Treat Programs as%of All Admits 94'	38	7.2447
CPC149 'Expend for State-Supported Alcohol&Drug Abuse Services:94'	50	7.9E+07
CPC150 'Per Capita Expend for State-Supported Alc&Drug Abuse Services 94'	50	14.5820
CPC151 'Expend for State-Supported Alcohol&Drug Abuse Treat Programs 94'	50	6.2E+07
CPC152 'Expend per Alcohol&Drug Treat Admission 1994'	50	1481.68
CPC153 'Per Capita Expend for State-Supported Alcohol&Drug Abuse Prog 94'	50	11.7014
CPC154 'Expend for State-Supported Alcohol&Drug Abuse Prevent Programs 94	50	1.1E+07
CPC155 'Per Capita Expend for State-Supported Alcohol& Drug Abuse Prog 94'	50	1.9410
CPC157 'Per Capita State&Local Gvt Expend for Justice Activities:1993'	51	301.7675
CPC158 'State&Loc Gvt Expend for Justice Activities as%of all Expend 93'	51	6.2237
CPC166 'Per Capita State&Local Gvt Expend for Police Protection:1993'	51	130.4298
CPC175 'Per Capita State&Loc Gvt Expend for Corrections 1993'	51	107.0467
CPC184 'Per Capita State&Loc Gvt Expend for Judicial&Legal Services 1993'	51	64.2918
CPC185 'State&LocGvt Expend for Judicial&Legal Services as%of Expend 93'	51	1.3092
CPC47 'Prisoners in State Correctional Institutions 1996'	51	20796.7
CPC48 'State Prisoner Incarceration Rate 1996'	51	350.3529
CPC49 'Prisoners in State Correctional Institutions 1995'	51	19727.2
CPC51 'State Prison Population as%of Highest Capacity 1995'	50	113.1400
CPC52 'Prisoners in State Correctional Institutions:Year End 1995'	51	20114.2
CPC56 'Female Prisoners in State Correctional Institutions 1995'	51	1198.94
CPC57 'Female State Prisoner Incarceration Rate 1995'	51	38.0784
CPC60 'White Prisoners in State Correctional Institut 1994'	51	7956.16
CPC61 'White State Prisoner Incarceration Rate 1994'	51	181.0000
CPC63 'Black Prisoners in State Correctional Institut 1994'	51	9180.86
CPC64 'Black State Prisoner Incarceration Rate 1994'	50	1446.00
CPC68 'Prisoners Under Sentence of Death 1995'	38	80.1579
CPC69 'Male Prisoners Under Sentence of Death 1995'	38	78.8947
CPC70 'Female Prisoners Under Sentence of Death 1995'	38	1.2632
CPC71 '% of Prisoners Under Sentence of Death Who Are Female:1995'	38	.8734
CPC72 'White Prisoners Under Sentence of Death 1995'	38	45.4474
CPC73 '% of Prisoners Under Sentence of Death Who Are White:1995'	38	55.4755
CPC74 'Black Prisoners Under Sentence of Death 1995'	38	33.4211
CPC75 '% of Prisoners Under Sentence of Death Who Are Black:1995'	38	32.4411
CPC76 'Prisoners Executed:1930-95'	51	81.1569
CPC77 'Prisoners Executed:1977-95'	51	6.1373
CPC78 'Prisoners Sentenced to Death:1973-95'	40	139.2750
CPC79 'Death Sentences Overturned or Commuted:1973-95'	40	51.1250
CPC80 '% of Death Penalty Sentences Overturned or Commuted:1973-95'	40	42.9218

Descriptive Statistics

	N	Mean
CPC81 'Prisoners Admitted to State Correctional Institut 1994'	50	10282.2
CPC96 'Death Rate of State Prisoners 1994'	50	290.5600
CPC98 'Deaths State Prisoners:Illness,Natural Cause as%of Prison Deaths 94'	46	60.1502
CPC99 'Deaths of State Prisoners by AIDS 1994'	48	19.8958
CRC310 'Crimes 1995'	51	271905
CRC314 'Crime Rate 1995'	51	5142.95
CRC316 'Violent Crimes 1995'	51	35270.3
CRC320 'Violent Crime Rate 1995'	51	581.0196
CRC325 'Bombings 1995'	51	38.0588
CRC326 'Murders 1995'	51	423.4706
CRC329 'Murder Rate 1995'	51	7.8549
CRC345 'Rapes 1995'	51	1911.06
CRC348 'Rape Rate 1995'	51	37.8824
CRC351 'Robberies 1995'	51	11383.2
CRC354 'Robbery Rate 1995'	51	174.0765
CRC366 'Aggravated Assaults 1995'	51	21552.5
CRC369 'Aggravated Assault Rate 1995'	51	361.1922
CRC380 'Property Crimes 1995'	51	236634
CRC384 'Property Crime Rate 1995'	51	4561.94
CRC386 'Burglaries 1995'	51	50882.3
CRC389 'Burglary Rate 1995'	51	944.1882
CRC391 'Larcenies&Thefts 1995'	51	156875
CRC394 'Larceny&Theft Rate 1995'	51	3138.93
CRC396 'Motor Vehicle Thefts 1995'	51	28877.1
CRC399 'Motor Vehicle Theft Rate 1995'	51	478.8098
CRC401 'Crime in Urban Areas 1995'	48	258632
CRC402 'Urban Crime Rate 1995'	48	5771.59
CRC404 'Crime in Rural Areas 1995'	48	13248.3
CRC405 'Rural Crime Rate 1995'	48	2089.30
CRC461 'Crimes Reported at Univ&Colleges 1995'	42	2738.64
CRC462 'Crimes Reported at Univer&Colleges as%of All Crimes 1995'	42	1.0340
CRC463 'Violent Crimes Reported at Univ&Colleges 1994'	42	69.2857
CRC464 'Violent Crimes Reported at Univ&Colleges as%of Violent Crimes 95'	42	.2798
CRC465 'Property Crimes Reported at Universities&Colleges 1995'	42	2669.36
CRC466 'Property Crimes at Univ&Colleges as%of All Property Crimes 95'	42	1.1231
CRC507 'Hate Crimes 1995'	46	172.7609
CRC508 'Rate of Reported Hate Crimes 1995'	46	4.6065
DMC509 'Population 1996'	51	5201647
DMC510 'Population 1995'	51	5154725
DMC511 'Population 1991'	51	4943314
DMC512 'Urban Population 1995'	48	4529346
DMC513 'Rural Population 1995'	48	626674
DMC514 'Population 10 to 17 Years Old 1995'	51	586840
DMS390 'Households 1995'	51	1903137
Valid N (listwise)	35	

Descriptive Statistics

	N	Mean
DMS391 '% Change in Households: 1990 to 95'	51	6.2098
DMS392 'Persons per Households 1995'	51	2.6161
DMS393 'Family Households 1990'	51	1265058
DMS394 'Married-Couple Family Households 1990'	51	994281
DMS395 'Married-Couple Family Households as a % of Households 1990'	51	55.9529
DMS415 'Population 1996'	51	5201647
DMS418 'Population Change: 1990 to 96'	51	324813
DMS423 'Resident State Population 1990'	51	4876829
DMS425 'Resident State Population in 1980'	51	4442075
DMS426 'Resident State Population in 1970'	51	3986275
DMS427 'Resident State Population in 1960'	51	3516118
DMS428 'Resident State Population in 1950'	51	2967173
DMS429 'Projected State Population in 2005'	51	5607451
DMS430 'Projected Population Change: 1995 to 2005'	51	455412
DMS431 'Projected % Change in Population: 1995 to 2005'	51	10.2086
DMS432 'Population per Square Mile 1996'	51	343.8796
DMS438 'Urban Population 1990'	51	3667715
DMS439 '% of Population Urban 1990'	51	68.8039
DMS440 'Rural Population 1990'	51	1208949
DMS441 '% of Population Rural 1990'	51	31.1961
DMS442 'Metropolitan Population 1994'	51	4071667
DMS443 '% of Population Living in a Metropolitan Area 1994'	51	67.6137
DMS444 'Nonmetropolitan Population 1994'	51	1033020
DMS445 '% of Population Living in a Nonmetropolitan Area 1994'	51	32.3471
DMS446 'Male Population 1995'	51	2515957
DMS447 'Female Population 1995'	51	2636107
DMS448 'White Population 1995'	51	4275118
DMS449 '% of Population White 1995'	51	84.1194
DMS450 'Black Population 1995'	51	649569
DMS451 '% of Population Black 1995'	51	11.0341
DMS452 'Hispanic Population 1995'	51	527863
DMS453 '% of Population Hispanic 1995'	51	6.0592
DMS454 'Asian Population 1995'	51	183314
DMS455 '% of Population Asian 1995'	51	3.2125
DMS456 'American Indian Population 1995'	51	43843.1
DMS457 '% of Population American Indian 1995'	51	1.6173
DMS458 'Projected White Population in 2005'	51	4558118
DMS459 'Projected % of Population White in 2005'	51	82.8020
DMS460 'Projected Black Population in 2005'	51	740020
DMS461 'Projected % of Population Black in 2005'	51	11.5490
DMS462 'Projected Hispanic Population in 2005'	51	707039
DMS463 'Projected % of Population Hispanic in 2005'	51	7.4431
DMS464 'Projected Asian Population in 2005'	51	259059
DMS465 'Projected % of Population Asian in 2005'	51	3.9647

Descriptive Statistics

	N	Mean
DMS466 'Projected American Indian Population in 2005'	51	50215.7
DMS467 'Projected % of Population American Indian in 2005'	51	1.6627
DMS468 'Median Age 1995'	51	33.9157
DMS469 'Population Under 5 Years Old 1995'	51	384140
DMS470 'Population 5 to 17 Years Old 1995'	51	963702
DMS471 'Population 18 Years Old and Older 1995'	51	3804222
DMS472 '% of Population 18 Years Old and Older 1995'	51	73.7329
DMS473 'Population 18 to 24 Years Old 1995'	51	488869
DMS474 'Population 25 to 44 Years Old 1995'	51	1634134
DMS475 'Population 45 to 64 Years Old 1995'	51	1023722
DMS476 'Population 65 Years Old and Older 1995'	51	657496
DMS477 '% of Population 65 Years Old and Older 1995'	51	12.7078
DMS478 'Population 85 Years Old and Older 1995'	51	71140.3
DMS479 '% of Population 85 Years Old and Older 1995'	51	1.4041
DMS490 'Marriage Rate 1995'	51	10.5235
DMS492 'Divorce Rate 1995'	47	4.6766
EES100 Projected Gross State Product in 2005	51	1.3E+11
EES101 Projected Avg Ann Growth in Gross State Product:1992-2005	51	2.2608
EES106 Personal Income 1995	51	1.2E+11
EES108 Per Capita Personal Income 1995	51	22388.8
EES110 Projected Per Capita Personal Income in 2005	51	18205.7
EES111 Projected Avg Ann Growth in Per Cap Personal Income:93-2005	51	1.2529
EES112 Adjusted Gross Income 1993	51	7.2E+10
EES113 Per Capita Adjusted Gross Income 1993	51	13958.9
EES114 Median Household Income 1995	51	33814.1
EES396 'Housing Units 1995'	51	2118176
EES398 'Homeownership Rate 1996'	51	66.8431
EES399 '% Change in Homeownership Rate: 86 to 96'	51	2.3355
EES400 'Median Value of a House 1990'	51	84209.8
EES401 'Median Mthly Mortgage Payment for OwnerOcc HousingUnits 90'	51	723.2941
EES410 'Median Monthly Rent Payment 1990'	51	349.6471
EES411 'Mobile Homes and Trailers 1990'	51	167079
EES412 '% of Housing Units Without a Telephone 1990'	51	4.9710
EES413 'State&Loc Gvt Expend for Housing & Community Development 93'	51	3.6E+08
EES414 'PerCapita State&LocGvt Expend Housing&Commnty Develop 93'	51	68.7463
EES96 Gross State Product 1992	51	1.2E+11
EES97 % Change in Gross State Product: 1982 to 92	51	90.6890
EES98 Per Capita Gross State Product 1992	51	23982.1
EES99 % Change in Per Capita Gross State Product: 1982 to 92	51	74.9425
ENS192 Energy Consumption 1994	51	1.7E+15
ENS193 Per Capita Energy Consumption 1994	51	3.8E+08
ENS209 'Power Plants 1996'	51	60.6667
ENS210 'Nuclear Power Plants 1996'	51	1.3529
ENS211 'Hazardous Waste Sites on the National Priority List 1996'	51	24.8039

Descriptive Statistics

	N	Mean
ENS212 'Hazardous Waste Sites National Priority List Per10k SqMI 96'	51	11.3876
ENS213 'Pollution Released by Manufacturing Plants 1994'	51	4.4E+07
ENS214 '%Change in Pollution Released by Manufacturing Plants:93-94'	50	-7.7828
ENS215 'Wetlands in 80's'	50	5488522
ENS216 '% of Surface Area That Are Wetlands in 80's'	50	7.8700
ENS217 '% of Wetlands Lost: 1780's to 80's'	50	48.3820
ENS231 'Tornadoes 1995'	51	24.3529
ENS232 'Tornadoes: 50 to 95'	51	699.5098
ENS233 'Fatalities Caused by Tornadoes: 50 to 95'	51	81.2353
ENS234 'Cost of Damage Caused by Tornadoes: 50 to 95'	51	3.6E+08
ENS239 'Acres of Land Owned by the Federal Gvt 1994'	51	1.3E+07
ENS240 '% of Land Owned by the Federal Gvt 1994'	51	16.7522
HTS325 'Persons Not Covered by Health Insurance 1995'	51	791019
HTS326 '% of Population Not Covered by Health Insurance 1995'	51	14.1549
HTS327 'Personal Health Care Expenditures 1993'	51	1.5E+10
HTS328 'Per Capita Personal Health Care Expenditures 1993'	51	2955.41
HTS329 'Nonfederal Physicians 1995'	51	13512.2
HTS330 'Rate of Nonfederal Physicians 1995'	51	253.2745
HTS331 'Community Hospitals 1995'	51	101.8431
HTS332 'Community Hospitals per 100,000 Population 1995'	51	2.5973
HTS333 'Births 1995'	51	76472.4
HTS334 'Birth Rate 1995'	51	14.3804
HTS335 'Births to White Women 1995'	51	60888.5
HTS336 'Births to Black Women 1995'	51	11736.4
HTS337 'Births of Low Birthweight 1995'	51	5552.49
HTS338 'Births of Low Birthweight as a % of All Births 1995'	51	7.2490
HTS339 'Teenage Birth Rate 1994'	51	55.9098
HTS340 'Births to Unmarried Women as a % of All Births 1995'	50	31.1900
HTS341 'Births Unmarried White Women as%of Births to Whites 95'	50	23.6660
HTS342 'Births Unmarried Black Women as% of Births to Blacks 95'	49	63.4429
HTS343 'Fertility Rate 1995'	51	63.6745
HTS344 '% of Mothers Receiving Late or No Prenatal Care 1994'	51	4.1216
HTS345 'Reported Legal Abortions 1992'	51	26649.9
HTS346 'Reported Legal Abortions per 1,000 Live Births 1992'	50	257.5600
HTS347 'Infant Deaths 1995'	51	574.6275
HTS348 'Infant Mortality Rate 1995'	50	7.4820
HTS349 'White Infant Mortality Rate 1994'	50	6.6140
HTS350 'Black Infant Mortality Rate 1994'	36	16.1278
HTS351 'Deaths 1995'	51	45336.8
HTS352 'Death Rate 1995'	51	883.0294
HTS353 'Age-Adjusted Death Rate 1995'	51	503.2784
HTS354 'Deaths by Accidents 1994'	51	1792.88
HTS355 'Death Rate by Accidents 1994'	51	37.5961
HTS356 'Alcohol-Induced Deaths 1994'	51	395.3529

Descriptive Statistics

	N	Mean
HTS357 'Death Rate from Alcohol-Induced Deaths 1994'	51	7.8573
HTS358 'Estimated Deaths by Cancer 1997'	51	10982.9
HTS359 'Estimated Age-Adjusted Death Rate by Cancer 1997'	51	171.5686
HTS360 'Estimated New Cancer Cases 1997'	51	27111.8
HTS361 'Estimated Rate of New Cancer Cases 1997'	51	523.9627
HTS362 'Deaths by Cerebrovascular Diseases 1994'	51	3006.00
HTS363 'Death Rate by Cerebrovascular Diseases 1994'	51	60.0608
HTS364 'Deaths by Chronic Liver Disease and Cirrhosis 1994'	51	498.1569
HTS365 'Death Rate by Chronic Liver Disease and Cirrhosis 1994'	51	9.2686
HTS366 'Deaths by Chronic Obstructive Pulmonary Diseases 1994'	51	1992.71
HTS367 'Death Rate by Chronic Obstructive Pulmonary Diseases 1994'	51	40.3569
HTS368 'Deaths by Diabetes Mellitus 1994'	51	1111.61
HTS369 'Death Rate by Diabetes Mellitus 1994'	51	21.8902
HTS370 'Deaths by Diseases of the Heart 1994'	51	14361.0
HTS371 'Death Rate by Diseases of the Heart 1994'	51	274.1353
HTS372 'Drug-Induced Deaths 1994'	51	273.0000
HTS373 'Death Rate from Drug-Induced Deaths 1994'	51	4.7482
HTS374 'Deaths by Injury 1994'	51	2763.53
HTS375 'Death Rate by Injury 1994'	51	60.9337
HTS376 'Deaths by Malignant Neoplasms 1994'	51	10476.7
HTS377 'Death Rate by Malignant Neoplasms 1994'	51	204.6980
HTS378 'Deaths by Pneumonia and Influenza 1994'	51	1597.51
HTS379 'Death Rate by Pneumonia and Influenza 1994'	51	31.1039
HTS380 'Deaths by Suicide 1994'	51	610.6275
HTS381 'Death Rate by Suicide 1994'	51	13.0176
HTS382 'Deaths by AIDS Through 94'	51	4310.63
HTS383 'Deaths by AIDS 1994'	51	825.7647
HTS384 'Death Rate by AIDS 1994'	48	13.5333
HTS385 'AIDS Cases Reported 1996'	51	1374.57
HTS386 'AID Rate 1996'	51	21.5941
HTS387 'AIDS Cases Reported Through June 96'	51	10392.1
HTS388 'Adult Per Capita Apparent Alcohol Consumption 1995'	51	2.5273
HTS389 '% of Adults Who Smoke 1995'	50	22.7048
JBS158 Avg Annual Pay 1995	51	26256.7
JBS159 % Change in Avg Annual Pay: 1994 to 95	51	3.2784
JBS160 State Minimum Wage Rates 1997	43	4.4865
JBS161 Avg Hrly Earnings Production Workers on Manufact Payrolls 96	50	12.6310
JBS162 Avg Wkly Earnings Production Workers on Manufact Payrolls 96	50	527.1316
JBS163 Avg Work Week of Production Workers on Manufact Payrolls 96	50	41.6240
JBS164 Workers Compensation Benefit Payments 1993	51	7.8E+08
JBS165 Workers Compensation Benefit Payment per Employee 1993	51	324.7206
JBS167 Civilian Labor Force 1996	51	2644357
JBS168 Employed Civilian Labor Force 1996	51	2509222
JBS169 Unemployed Civilian Labor Force 1996	51	135135

Descriptive Statistics

	N	Mean
JBS170 Unemployment Rate 1996	51	4.8647
JBS171 Women in Civilian Labor Force 1995	51	1194784
JBS172 % of Women in the Civilian Labor Force 1995	51	60.6510
JBS173 % of Civilian Labor Force Comprised of Women 1995	51	46.5647
JBS175 Employees on Nonfarm Payrolls 1996	51	2358575
JBS176 Employees in Construction 1996	51	105559
JBS177 % of Nonfarm Employees in Construction 1996	51	4.7047
JBS178 Employees in Finance, Insurance and Real Estate 1996	51	134682
JBS179 % of Nonfarm Employees in Finance, Insur & Real Estate 1996	51	5.3910
JBS180 Employees in Gvt 1996	51	388982
JBS181 % of Nonfarm Employees in Gvt 1996	51	17.8453
JBS182 Employees in Manufacturing 1996	51	361249
JBS183 % of Nonfarm Employees in Manufacturing 1996	51	14.4335
JBS184 Employees in Mining 1996	51	11609.8
JBS185 % of Nonfarm Employees in Mining 1996	51	.8453
JBS186 Employees in Service Industries 1996	51	675112
JBS187 % of Nonfarm Employees in Service Industries 1996	51	27.9816
JBS188 Employees in Transportation and Public Utilities 1996	51	122176
JBS189 % of Nonfarm Employees in Transportation & Public Utility 96	51	5.1833
JBS190 Employees in Wholesale and Retail Trade 1996	51	559614
JBS191 % of Nonfarm Employees in Wholesale and Retail Trade 1996	51	23.6927
PVS501 'Poverty Rate 1995'	51	13.1216
PVS502 '% of School Age Children Living in Poverty 1995'	51	17.5333
PVS503 'State&Loc Gvt Expend for Public Welfare Programs 1993'	51	3.3E+09
PVS504 'PerCapita State&Loc Gvt Expend PublicWelfare Programs 93'	51	629.5061
PVS505 'State&Loc Gvt Spending Welfare Prog as%ofState&Loc Exp 93'	51	13.4951
PVS506 '% of Population Receiving Public Aid 1994'	51	6.8725
PVS508 'Per Capita Social Security (OASDI) Payments 1995'	51	1244.81
PVS511 'Avg Monthly Social Security (OASDI) Payment 1995'	51	641.3280
PVS514 'Medicare Payments per Enrollee 1995'	51	4514.69
PVS515 '% of Population Enrolled in Medicare 1995'	51	14.1245
PVS522 '% of Population Receiving Food Stamps 1995'	51	9.6443
PVS523 'Avg Monthly Food Stamp Benefit per Recipient 1995'	51	70.6002
PVS525 '% of Households Receiving Food Stamps 1995'	51	10.5757
PVS526 'Avg Monthly Food Stamp Benefit per Household 1995'	51	173.1653
PVS528 'Per Capita AFDC Costs 95'	51	80.5810
PVS531 'Avg Monthly AFDC Payment per Recipient Family 1995'	51	344.4802
PVS537 'Avg Cost of National Schl Lunch ProgramPerParticipnt 96'	51	192.8427
PVS538 '% of Schls Partic in Both Fed Schl Lunch& Breakfast Prog 96'	51	71.1667
PVS539 '% of Low-Inc Students Partic Fed Schl Lunch&Breakfast Prog 96'	51	36.5471
REGION4 Census Region 4 Dvisions	51	2.6667
REGION9 Census Regions 9 Divisions	51	5.1961
SCS121 Public Elementary and Secondary School Districts 1995	51	289.6471
SCS122 Public Elementary and Secondary Schools 1995	51	1690.61

Descriptive Statistics

	N	Mean
SCS123 School-Age Population as a % of Total Population 1995	51	19.0451
SCS124 Enrollment in Public Elementary and Secondary Schools 1996	51	874937
SCS125 % of Elem & Sec School Students in Private Schools 1994	51	9.2065
SCS126 Enrollment in Public Elementary Schools (Grades K-8) 1996	51	572076
SCS127 Enrollment in Public Secondary Schools (Grades 9-12) 1996	51	302861
SCS128 Pupil-Teacher Ratio in Public Elem & Secondary Schools 1995	51	16.6373
SCS129 Teachers in Public Elementary and Secondary Schools 1996	51	50661.0
SCS130 Avg Salary of Classroom Teachers 1996	51	36027.2
SCS131 Public High School Graduates 1996	51	45190.6
SCS132 % Change in Public High School Graduates: 1991 to 96	51	3.4843
SCS133 Public High School Graduation Rate 1994	51	73.7529
SCS134 High School Drop Out Rate 1990	51	10.3804
SCS135 % of Population Graduated from High School as of 95	51	82.7510
SCS136 Education Expenditures by State and Local Gvts 1993	51	6.7E+09
SCS137 Per Capita State&Loc Gvt Expenditures for Education 1993	51	1356.68
SCS138 Expend for Education as % of all State&Loc Gvt Expend 1993	51	29.6751
SCS139 Elem and Sec Education Expenditures by State&Loc Gvts 1993	51	4.7E+09
SCS140 Per Capita State&Loc Gvt Expend for Elem&Sec Education 1993	51	932.1404
SCS141 Expend for Elem & Sec Education as % of all State&Loc Gvt 96	51	20.2314
SCS142 Expenditures per Pupil in Elem and Sec Schools 1996	51	5616.84
SCS143 Higher Education Expenditures by State and Local Gvts 1993	51	1.7E+09
SCS144 Per Capita State&Loc Gvt Expenditures for Higher Educ 1993	51	366.4518
SCS145 Expend for Higher Educ as% of all State&Loc Gvt Expend 94	51	8.1369
SCS146 Avg Undergrad Tuition,Fees,Rm,Brd, Public Instit HigherEd 96	49	6891.12
SCS147 Avg Undergrad Tuition,Fees,Rm,Brd,Private Instit HigherEd 96	49	15693.5
SCS148 Institutions of Higher Education 1996	51	72.4706
SCS149 Enrollment in Institutions of Higher Education 1994	51	278967
SCS150 Enrollment in Public Institutions of Higher Education 1994	51	217298
SCS151 Enrollment in Private Institutions of Higher Education 1994	51	61668.8
SCS152 % of Population Graduated from College as of 1995	51	22.8627
SCS153 Public Libraries and Branches 1993	51	311.8431
SCS154 Public Libraries and Branches per 10,000 Population 1993	51	.8865
SCS155 Books in Public Libraries Per Capita 1993	51	2.9627
SCS156 Enrollment in Head Start Program 1995	51	12887.0
SCS157 Federal Allocations for Head Start Program 1995	51	5.9E+07
ST STATE CODE	51	26.00
TXS241 'Internal Revenue Service Collections 1995'	50	2.7E+10
TXS242 'Federal Individual Income and Employment Tax Collections 95'	50	2.3E+10
TXS244 'Federal Corporate Income Tax Collections 1995'	50	3.4E+09
TXS267 'Per Capita State and Local Gvt Revenue 1993'	51	5019.55
TXS294 'State Tobacco Product Sales Tax Revenue 1995'	51	1.4E+08
TXS295 'Per Capita State Tobacco Sales Tax Revenue 1995'	51	26.8075
TXS296 'State Tax on a Pack of Cigarettes 1996'	51	33.7627
TXS297 'State Alcoholic Beverage Sales Tax Revenue 1995'	51	7.1E+07

Descriptive Statistics

	N	Mean
TXS298 'Per Capita State Alcoholic Beverage Sales Tax Revenue 1995'	51	13.4943
TXS299 'State Lottery Net Income 1994'	36	2.7E+08
TXS300 'Per Capita State Lottery Net Income 1994'	36	40.2606
TXS324 'Avg Annual Earnings Full-Time State&Loc Gvt Employees 94'	51	31105.6
VTS497 'Registered Voters 1994'	51	2314591
VTS498 '% of Eligible Voters Reported Registered 1994'	51	65.3490
VTS499 'Persons Voting 1994'	51	1665621
VTS500 '% of Eligible Population Reported Voting 1994'	51	47.3451
WWS78 U.S. Dept of Defense Expenditures 1995	51	4.1E+09
WWS79 Per Capita U.S. Dept of Defense Expenditures 1995	51	889.9884
WWS80 U.S. Dept of Defense Total Contracts for 1995	51	2.1E+09
WWS81 Per Capita U.S. Dept of Defense Contracts 1995	51	412.6108
WWS93 Veterans 1996	51	504941
WWS94 Veterans per 1,000 Population 18 and Older 1996	51	136.6392
WWS95 Veterans of the Persian Gulf War 1996	51	32333.3

APPENDIX 2: GSS96.SAV FILE INFORMATION

```
Name
ID            RESPONDENT ID NUMBER

ABANY         ABORTION IF WOMAN WANTS FOR ANY REASON
              Please tell me whether or not you think it should be possible for a pregnant
              woman to obtain a legal abortion if...the woman wants it for any reason?
              Missing Values: 0, 9
              Value     Label
                 0 M    NAP
                 1      YES
                 2      NO
                 8      DK
                 9 M    NA

ABDEFECT      STRONG CHANCE OF SERIOUS DEFECT
              Please tell me whether or not you think it should be possible for a pregnant
              woman to obtain a legal abortion if...there is a strong chance of serious
              defect in the baby?
              Missing Values: 0, 9
              Value     Label
                 0 M    NAP
                 1      YES
                 2      NO
                 8      DK
                 9 M    NA

ABHLTH        WOMANS HEALTH SERIOUSLY ENDANGERED
              Please tell me whether or not you think it should be possible for a pregnant
              woman to obtain a legal abortion if...the woman's health is seriously
              endangered by the pregnancy?
              Missing Values: 0, 9
              Value     Label
                 0 M    NAP
                 1      YES
                 2      NO
                 8      DK
                 9 M    NA

ABNOMORE      MARRIED--WANTS NO MORE CHILDREN
              Please tell me whether or not you think it should be possible for a pregnant
              woman to obtain a legal abortion if...she is married and does not want any
              more children?
              Missing Values: 0, 9
              Value     Label
                 0 M    NAP
                 1      YES
                 2      NO
                 8      DK
                 9 M    NA
```

ABPOOR   LOW INCOME--CANT AFFORD MORE CHILDREN
            Please tell me whether or not you think it should be possible for a pregnant
            woman to obtain a legal abortion if...the family has a very low income and
            cannot afford any more children?
            Missing Values: 0, 9
            Value   Label
              0 M   NAP
              1   YES
              2   NO
              8   DK
              9 M   NA

ABRAPE   PREGNANT AS RESULT OF RAPE
            Please tell me whether or not you think it should be possible for a pregnant
            woman to obtain a legal abortion if...she became pregnant as a result of
            rape?
            Missing Values: 0, 9
            Value   Label
              0 M   NAP
              1   YES
              2   NO
              8   DK
              9 M   NA

AFFRMACT   FAVOR PREFERENCE IN HIRING BLACKS
            Some people say that because of past discrimination, blacks should be given
            preference in hiring and promotion. Others say that such a preference in
            hiring and promotion of blacks is wrong because it discriminates against
            whites. What about your opinion — are you for or against preferential hiring
            and promotion of blacks?
            Missing Values: 0, 9
            Value   Label
              0 M   NAP
              1   STRONGLY SUPPORT PREF
              2   SUPPORT PREF
              3   OPPOSE PREF
              4   STRONGLY OPPOSE PREF
              8   DK
              9 M   NA

AGE   AGE OF RESPONDENT
            Missing Values: 0, 99, 98
            Value   Label
             98 M   DK
             99 M   NA

AIDCOL   GOV. SHOULD ASSIST LOW-INCOME COLLEGE STUDENT
             On the whole, do you think it should or should not be the government's
             responsibility to...give financial assistance to college students from low-
             income families?
             Missing Values: 0, 9
             Value   Label
                 0 M   NAP
                 1   DEFIN SHOULD BE
                 2   PROBAB SHOULD BE
                 3   PROB SHOULD NOT BE
                 4   DEFIN SHOULD NOT BE
                 8   CANT CHOOSE
                 9 M   NA

AIDHOUSE   GOV. SHOULD PROVIDE HOUSING TO POOR
             On the whole, do you think it should or should not be the government's
             responsibility to...provide decent housing for those who can't afford it?
             Missing Values: 0, 9
             Value   Label
                 0 M   NAP
                 1   DEFIN SHOULD BE
                 2   PROBAB SHOULD BE
                 3   PROB SHOULD NOT BE
                 4   DEFIN SHOULD NOT BE
                 8   CANT CHOOSE
                 9 M   NA

AIDOLD   GOVTS RESP: PROVIDE FOR THE ELDERLY.
             On the whole, do you think it should or should not be the government's
             responsibility to...provide a decent standard of living for the old?
             Missing Values: 0, 9
             Value   Label
                 0 M   NAP
                 1   DEFIN SHOULD BE
                 2   PROBAB SHOULD BE
                 3   PROB SHOULD NOT BE
                 4   DEFIN SHOULD NOT BE
                 8   CANT CHOOSE
                 9 M   NA

AIDUNEMP   GOVTS RESP: PROVIDE FOR THE UNEMPLOYED.
             On the whole, do you think it should or should not be the government's
             responsibility to...provide a decent standard of living for the unemployed?
             Missing Values: 0, 9
             Value   Label
                 0 M   NAP
                 1   DEFIN SHOULD BE
                 2   PROBAB SHOULD BE
                 3   PROB SHOULD NOT BE
                 4   DEFIN SHOULD NOT BE
                 8   CANT CHOOSE
                 9 M   NA

AMBETTER Agree America is a better country
     How much do you agree or disagree that...generally speaking, America is a
     better country than most other countries?
     Missing Values: 0, 9
     Value   Label
       0 M NAP
       1   Strongly agree
       2   Agree
       3   Neither agree nor disagree
       4   Disagree
       5   Strongly disagree
       8   Cant choose
       9 M NA

AMCHRSTN How important to be a Christian
     Some people say the following things are important for being truly American.
     Athers say they are not important. How important do you think it is...to be
     a christian?
     Missing Values: 0, 9
     Value   Label
       0 M NAP
       1   Very important
       2   Fairly important
       3   Not very important
       4   Not important at all
       8   Cant choose
       9 M NA

AMSHAMED Agree There are things make me ashamed
     How much do you agree or disagree that...there are some things about America
     today that make me fell ashamed of America.
     Missing Values: 0, 9
     Value   Label
       0 M NAP
       1   Strongly agree
       2   Agree
       3   Neither agree nor disagree
       4   Disagree
       5   Strongly disagree
       8   Cant choose
       9 M NA

AMSPORTS Agree sports makes me proud to be an American
     How much do you agree or disagree that...when my country does well in
     international sports, it makes me proud to be an American?
     Missing Values: 0, 9
     Value   Label
       0 M NAP
       1   Strongly agree
       2   Agree
       3   Neither agree nor disagree
       4   Disagree
       5   Strongly disagree
       8   Cant choose
       9 M NA

ATTEND   HOW OFTEN R ATTENDS RELIGIOUS SERVICES
          How often do you attend religious services?
          Missing Values: 9
          Value   Label
              0   NEVER
              1   LT ONCE A YEAR
              2   ONCE A YEAR
              3   SEVRL TIMES A YR
              4   ONCE A MONTH
              5   2-3X A MONTH
              6   NRLY EVERY WEEK
              7   EVERY WEEK
              8   MORE THN ONCE WK
              9 M   DK,NA

BADBRKS   Most of my problems are due to bad breaks.
          The following are statements that people have made. For each one, please
          tell me if you strongly agree, disagree or strongly disagree with the
          statement...most of my problems are due to bad breaks.
          Missing Values: 0, 9
          Value   Label
              0 M   NAP
              1   strongly agree
              2   agree
              3   NEITHER AGREE OR DISAGREE-IT DEPENDS
              4   disagree
              5   strongly disagree
              8   DONT KNOW
              9 M   NA

BELIKEUS Agree better if people were more like Americans
          How much do you agree or disagree with the following statement...the world
          would be a better place if people from other countries were more like the
          Americans?
          Missing Values: 0, 9
          Value   Label
              0 M   NAP
              1   Strongly agree
              2   Agree
              3   Neither agree nor disagree
              4   Disagree
              5   Strongly disagree
              8   Cant choose
              9 M   NA

CHILDS   NUMBER OF CHILDREN
          Missing Values: 9
          Value   Label
              8   EIGHT OR MORE
              9 M   NA

CLASS   SUBJECTIVE CLASS IDENTIFICATION
          If you were asked to use one of four names for your social class, which would
          you say you belong in: the lower class, the working class, the middle class,
          or the upper class?
          Missing Values: 0, 9
          Value   Label
            0 M NAP
            1   LOWER CLASS
            2   WORKING CLASS
            3   MIDDLE CLASS
            4   UPPER CLASS
            5   NO CLASS
            8   DK
            9 M NA

COHORT   YEAR OF BIRTH
          Missing Values: 0, 9999
          Value   Label
            0 M NAP
       9999 M NA

COLATH   ALLOW ANTI-RELIGIONIST TO TEACH
          There are always some people whose ideas are considered bad or dangerous by
          other people. For instance somebody who is against all churches and
          religion...should such a person be allowed to teach in a college or
          university or not?
          Missing Values: 0, 9
          Value   Label
            0 M NAP
            4   ALLOWED
            5   NOT ALLOWED
            8   DK
            9 M NA

COLCOM   SHOULD COMMUNIST TEACHER BE FIRED
          Now I would like to ask you some questions about a man who admits he is a
          communist...suppose he is teaching in a college. Should he be fired or not?
          Missing Values: 0, 9
          Value   Label
            0 M NAP
            4   FIRED
            5   NOT FIRED
            8   DK
            9 M NA

COLHOMO   ALLOW HOMOSEXUAL TO TEACH
          And what about a man who admits that he is homosexual...should such a person
          be allowed to teach in a college or university or not?
          Missing Values: 0, 9
          Value   Label
            0 M NAP
            4   ALLOWED
            5   NOT ALLOWED
            8   DK
            9 M NA

COLMIL   ALLOW MILITARIST TO TEACH
           Consider a person who advocates doing away with elections and letting the
           military run the country...should such a person be allowed to teach in a
           college or university or not?
           Missing Values: 0, 9
           Value   Label
               0 M   NAP
               4   ALLOWED
               5   NOT ALLOWED
               8   DK
               9 M   NA

COLRAC   ALLOW RACIST TO TEACH
           Or consider a person who believes that Blacks are genetically
           inferior...should such a person be allowed to teach in a college or
           university or not?
           Missing Values: 0, 9
           Value   Label
               0 M   NAP
               4   ALLOWED
               5   NOT ALLOWED
               8   DK
               9 M   NA

CONDOM   USED CONDOM LAST TIME
           The last time you had sex, was a condom used? By "sex" we mean vaginal, oral
           or anal sex.
           Missing Values: 0, 9
           Value   Label
               0 M   NAP
               1   Used last time
               2   Not used
               8   DK
               9 M   NA

DEGREE   RS HIGHEST DEGREE
           Missing Values: 7, 8, 9
           Value   Label
               0   LT HIGH SCHOOL
               1   HIGH SCHOOL
               2   JUNIOR COLLEGE
               3   BACHELOR
               4   GRADUATE
               7 M   NAP
               8 M   DK
               9 M   NA

DENOM   SPECIFIC DENOMINATION
           Missing Values: 0, 99
           Value   Label
               0 M   NAP
              10   AM BAPTIST ASSO
              11   AM BAPT CH IN USA
              12   NAT BAPT CONV OF AM
              13   NAT BAPT CONV USA
              14   SOUTHERN BAPTIST
              15   OTHER BAPTISTS

```
        18     BAPTIST-DK WHICH
        20     AFR METH EPISCOPAL
        21     AFR METH EP ZION
        22     UNITED METHODIST
        23     OTHER METHODIST
        28     METHODIST-DK WHICH
        30     AM LUTHERAN
        31     LUTH CH IN AMERICA
        32     LUTHERAN-MO SYNOD
        33     WI EVAN LUTH SYNOD
        34     OTHER LUTHERAN
        35     EVANGELICAL LUTH
        38     LUTHERAN-DK WHICH
        40     PRESBYTERIAN C IN US
        41     UNITED PRES CH IN US
        42     OTHER PRESBYTERIAN
        43     PRESBYTERIAN, MERGED
        48     PRESBYTERIAN-DK WH
        50     EPISCOPAL
        60     OTHER
        70     NO DENOMINATION
        98     DK
        99 M   NA
```

DISCAFF   WHITES HURT BY AFF. ACTION
           What do you think the chances are these days that a white person won't get a
           job or promotion while an equally qualified black person gets one instead.
           Is this very likely, somewhat likely, or not very likely to happen these
           days?
           Missing Values: 0, 9
           Value   Label
             0 M   NAP
             1   VERY LIKELY
             2   SOMEWHAT LIKELY
             3   NOT VERY LIKELY
             8   DONT KNOW
             9 M   NA

DISCAFFM   a man won't get a job or promotion
           What do you think the chances are these days that a man won't get a job or
           promotion while an equally or less qualified woman gets one instead? Is this
           very likely, somewhat likely, somewhat unlikely, or very unlikely these days?
           Missing Values: 0, 9
           Value   Label
             0 M   NAP
             1   Very likely
             2   Somewhat likely
             3   Somewhat unlikely
             4   Very unlikely
             8   DONT KNOW
             9 M   NA

DISCAFFW   a woman won't get a job or promotion
           What do you think the chances are these days that a woman won't get a job or
           promotion while an equally or less qualified man gets one instead? Is this
           very likely, somewhat likely, somewhat unlikely, or very unlikely these days?
           Missing Values: 0, 9
           Value   Label
               0 M NAP
               1   Very likely
               2   Somewhat likely
               3   Somewhat unlikely
               4   Very unlikely
               8   DONT KNOW
               9 M NA

DIVORCE   EVER BEEN DIVORCED OR SEPARATED
           Have you ever been divorced or legally separated?
           Missing Values: 0, 9
           Value   Label
               0 M NAP
               1   YES
               2   NO
               8   DK
               9 M NA

EDUC   HIGHEST YEAR OF SCHOOL COMPLETED
           Missing Values: 97, 99
           Value   Label
              97 M NAP
              98   DK
              99 M NA

EVPAIDSX   EVER HAVE SEX PAID FOR OR BEING PAID SINCE 18
           Thinking about the time since your 18th birthday, have you ever had sex with
           a person you paid or who paid you for sex?
           Missing Values: 0, 9
           Value   Label
               0 M NAP
               1   YES
               2   NO
               8   DK
               9 M NA

EVSTRAY   HAVE SEX OTHER THAN SPOUSE WHILE MARRIED
           Have you ever had sex with someone other than your husband or wife while you
           were married?
           Missing Values: 0, 9
           Value   Label
               0 M NAP
               1   YES
               2   NO
               3   NEVER MARRIED
               8   DK
               9 M NA

FEAR AFRAID TO WALK AT NIGHT IN NEIGHBORHOOD
  Is there any area right around here — that is, within a mile - where you
  would be afraid to walk alone at night?
  Missing Values: 0, 9
  Value Label
   0 M NAP
   1 YES
   2 NO
   8 DK
   9 M NA

FEHELP WIFE SHOULD HELP HUSBANDS CAREER FIRST
  Now I'm going to read several more statements. As I read each one, please
  tell me whether you strongly agree, agree, disagree, or strongly disagree
  with it. For example, here is the statement: it is important for a wife to
  help her husband's career than to have one herself.
  Missing Values: 0, 9
  Value Label
   0 M NAP
   1 STRONGLY AGREE
   2 AGREE
   3 DISAGREE
   4 STRONGLY DISAGREE
   8 DK
   9 M NA

FEIMP IMPORTANCE OF WOMENS RIGHTS ISSUE TO R
  How important is the women's rights issue to you — would you say it is one of
  the most important, important, not very important, or not important at all?
  Missing Values: 0, 9
  Value Label
   0 M NAP
   1 ONE OF MOST IMP
   2 IMPORTANT
   3 NOT VERY IMP
   4 NOT IMP AT ALL
   8 DK
   9 M NA

FEMINIST think yourself as a feminist?
  Do you think of yourself as a feminist or not?
  Missing Values: 0, 9
  Value Label
   0 M NAP
   1 Yes, a feminist
   2 No, not a feminist
   8 DONT KNOW
   9 M NA

FEPRES VOTE FOR WOMAN PRESIDENT
  If your party nominated a woman for President, would you vote for her if she
  were qualified for the job?
  Missing Values: 0, 9
  Value Label
   0 M NAP
   1 YES
   2 NO
   5 WOULDNT VOTE
   8 DK
   9 M NA

FEPRESCH   PRESCHOOL KIDS SUFFER IF MOTHER WORKS
           Now I'm going to read several more statements. As I read each one, please
           tell me whether you strongly agree, agree, disagree, or strongly disagree
           with it. For example, here is the statement: A preschool child is likely to
           suffer if his or her mother works.
           Missing Values: 0, 9
           Value   Label
               0 M   NAP
               1   STRONGLY AGREE
               2   AGREE
               3   DISAGREE
               4   STRONGLY DISAGREE
               8   DK
               9 M   NA

FEWORK   SHOULD WOMEN WORK
           Do you approve or disapprove of a married woman earning money in business or
           industry if she has a husband capable of supporting her?
           Missing Values: 0, 9
           Value   Label
               0 M   NAP
               1   APPROVE
               2   DISAPPROVE
               8   DK
               9 M   NA

GETAHEAD   OPINION OF HOW PEOPLE GET AHEAD
           Some people say that people get ahead by their own hard work: others say taht
           lucky breaks or help from other people are more important. Which do you
           think is more important?
           Missing Values: 0, 9
           Value   Label
               0 M   NAP
               1   HARD WORK
               2   BOTH EQUALLY
               3   LUCK OR HELP
               4   OTHER
               8   DK
               9 M   NA

GRASS   SHOULD MARIJUANA BE MADE LEGAL
           Do you think marijuana should be made legal or not?
           Missing Values: 0, 9
           Value   Label
               0 M   NAP
               1   LEGAL
               2   NOT LEGAL
               8   DK
               9 M   NA

HAPFEEL   Felt happy?
           Now I'm going to read a list of different feelings that people sometimes
           have. After each one, I would like you to tell me on how many days you have
           felt this way during the past seven days. Felt happy?
           Missing Values: *, 9
           Value   Label
              -1 M   NAP
               8   DK
               9 M   NA

HAPMAR   HAPPINESS OF MARRIAGE
        Taking things all together, how would you describe your marriage? Would you
        say that your marriage is very happy, pretty happy, or not too happy?
        Missing Values: 0, 9
        Value   Label

Value		Label
0	M	NAP
1		VERY HAPPY
2		PRETTY HAPPY
3		NOT TOO HAPPY
8		DK
9	M	NA

HOMOSEX   HOMOSEXUAL SEX RELATIONS
        What about sexual relations between two adults of the same sex — do you think
        it is always wrong, almost always wrong, wrong only sometimes, or not wrong
        at all?
        Missing Values: 0, 9

Value		Label
0	M	NAP
1		ALWAYS WRONG
2		ALMST ALWAYS WRG
3		SOMETIMES WRONG
4		NOT WRONG AT ALL
5		OTHER
8		DK
9	M	NA

HRS2   NUMBER OF HOURS USUALLY WORK A WEEK
        How many hours a week do you usually work, at all jobs?
        Missing Values: -1, 99, 98

Value		Label
-1	M	NAP
98	M	DK
99	M	NA

INCOME   TOTAL FAMILY INCOME
        Missing Values: 0, 99

Value		Label
0	M	NAP
1		LT $1000
2		$1000 TO 2999
3		$3000 TO 3999
4		$4000 TO 4999
5		$5000 TO 5999
6		$6000 TO 6999
7		$7000 TO 7999
8		$8000 TO 9999
9		$10000 - 14999
10		$15000 - 19999
11		$20000 - 24999
12		$25000 OR MORE
13		REFUSED
98		DK
99	M	NA

LABORPOW   POWER OF LABOR UNIONS IN RS COUNTRY.
            Do you think labor unions in this country have too much power or too little
            power?
            Missing Values: 0, 9
            Value   Label
                0 M   NAP
                1   FAR TOO MUCH POWER
                2   TOO MUCH POWER
                3   RIGHT AMNT OF POWER
                4   TOO LITTLE POWER
                5   FAR TOO LITTLE POWER
                8   CANT CHOOSE
                9 M   NA

LETDIE1   ALLOW INCURABLE PATIENTS TO DIE
            When a person has a disease that cannot be cured, do you think doctors should
            be allowed by law to end the patient's life by some painless means if the
            patient and the family request it?
            Missing Values: 0, 9
            Value   Label
                0 M   NAP
                1   YES
                2   NO
                8   DK
                9 M   NA

MARITAL   MARITAL STATUS
            What is your current marital status?
            Missing Values: 9
            Value   Label
                1   MARRIED
                2   WIDOWED
                3   DIVORCED
                4   SEPARATED
                5   NEVER MARRIED
                9 M   NA

MATESEX   WAS 1 OF RS PARTNERS SPOUSE OR REGULAR
            (Of the sexual partners you had in the last 12 months) was one of the
            partners your husband or wife or regular sexual partner?
            Missing Values: 0, 9
            Value   Label
                0 M   NAP
                1   YES
                2   NO
                8   DK
                9 M   NA

NEWS   HOW OFTEN DOES R READ NEWSPAPER
            How often do you read the newpaper — every day, a few times a week, once a
            week, less than once a week, or never?
            Missing Values: 0, 9
            Value   Label
                0 M   NAP
                1   EVERYDAY
                2   FEW TIMES A WEEK
                3   ONCE A WEEK
                4   LESS THAN ONCE WK
                5   NEVER
                8   DK
                9 M   NA

NOEMOTE   I keep my emotions to myself.
           The following are some statements that people have made. For each one tell
           me if you strongly agree, agree, disagree, or strongly disagree with the
           statement...I keep my emotions to myself.
           Missing Values: 0, 9
           Value   Label
               0 M NAP
               1   strongly agree
               2   agree
               3   NEITHER AGREE OR DISAGREE-IT DEPENDS
               4   disagree
               5   strongly disagree
               8   DONT KNOW
               9 M NA

NUMMEN   NUMBER OF MALE SEX PARTNERS SINCE 18
           Now thinking about the time since your 18th birthday (including the past 12
           months) how many male partners have you had sex with?
           Missing Values: 989 thru 999, -1
           Value   Label
              -1 M NAP
             989 M 989 OR HIGHER
             990 M DASH OR SLASH
             991 M SOME,1+
             992 M X
             993 M GARBLED TEXT
             994 M SEVERAL
             995 M MANY,LOTS
             996 M N.A
             997 M REFUSED
             998 M DK
             999 M NA

NUMWOMEN   NUMBER OF FEMALE SEX PARTNERS SINCE 18
           Now thinking about the time since your 18th birthday (including the past 12
           months) how many female partners have you had sex with?
           Missing Values: 989 thru 999, -1
           Value   Label
              -1 M NAP
             989 M 989 OR HIGHER
             990 M DASH OR SLASH
             991 M SOME,1+
             992 M X
             993 M GARBLED TEXT
             994 M SEVERAL
             995 M MANY,LOTS
             996 M N.A
             997 M REFUSED
             998 M DK
             999 M NA

PARSOL   RS LIVING STANDARD COMPARED TO PARENTS
           Compared to your parents when they were the age you are now, do you think
           your own standard of living now is much better, somewhat better, about the
           same, somewhat worse, or much worse than theirs was?
           Missing Values: 0, 9
           Value   Label
              0 M   NAP
              1   MUCH BETTER
              2   SOMEWHAT BETTER
              3   ABOUT THE SAME
              4   SOMEWHAT WORSE
              5   MUCH WORSE
              8   DK
              9 M   NA

PARTNERS   HOW MANY SEX PARTNERS R HAD IN LAST YEAR
           How many sex partners have you had in the last 12 months
           Missing Values: 95 thru 99, -1
           Value   Label
             -1 M   NAP
              0   NO PARTNERS
              1   1 PARTNER
              2   2 PARTNERS
              3   3 PARTNERS
              4   4 PARTNERS
              5   5-10 PARTNERS
              6   11-20 PARTNERS
              7   21-100 PARTNERS
              8   MORE THAN 100 PARTNERS
              9   1 OR MORE, DK #
             95 M   SEVERAL
             98 M   DK
             99 M   NA

POLEFF3   AVG PERSON CAN INFLUENCE POLITICIANS.
           Please indicate whether you agree or disagree with each of the following
           statmentes...the average citizen has considerable influence on politics.
           Missing Values: 0, 9
           Value   Label
              0 M   NAP
              1   Agree-Strongly Agree
              2   Disagree-Agree
              3   Neither Agree nor Disagree
              4   Disagree
              5   Strongly Disagree
              8   Can't Choose
              9 M   NA

POLVIEWS THINK OF SELF AS LIBERAL OR CONSERVATIVE
          We hear a lot of talk these days about liberals and conservatives. I'm going
          to show you a seven point scale on which the political views that people
          might hold are arranged from extremely liberal--point 1--to extremely
          concervative — point 7. Where would you place yourself on this scale?
          Missing Values: 0, 9
          Value   Label
             0 M   NAP
             1   EXTREMELY LIBERAL
             2   LIBERAL
             3   SLIGHTLY LIBERAL
             4   MODERATE
             5   SLGHTLY CONSERVATIVE
             6   CONSERVATIVE
             7   EXTRMLY CONSERVATIVE
             8   DK
             9 M   NA

PRAY   HOW OFTEN DOES R PRAY
          How often do you pray?
          Missing Values: 0, 9
          Value   Label
             0 M   NAP
             1   SEVERAL TIMES A DAY
             2   ONCE A DAY
             3   SEVERAL TIMES A WEEK
             4   ONCE A WEEK
             5   LT ONCE A WEEK
             6   NEVER
             8   DK
             9 M   NA

RACDIF1   DIFFERENCES DUE TO DISCRIMINATION
          On average Blacks have worse jobs, income, and housing than white people. Do
          you think these differences are mainly due to discrimination?
          Missing Values: 0, 9
          Value   Label
             0 M   NAP
             1   YES
             2   NO
             8   DK
             9 M   NA

RACDIF2   DIFFERENCES DUE TO INBORN DISABILITY
          On average Blacks have worse jobs, income, and housing than white people. Do
          you think these differences are mainly because Blacks have less in born
          ability to learn?
          Missing Values: 0, 9
          Value   Label
             0 M   NAP
             1   YES
             2   NO
             8   DK
             9 M   NA

RACDIF3   DIFFERENCES DUE TO LACK OF EDUCATION
           On average Blacks have worse jobs, income, and housing than white people. Do
           you think these differences are mainly because most Blacks don't have the
           chance for education that it takes to rise out of poverty?
           Missing Values: 0, 9
           Value   Label
               0 M NAP
               1   YES
               2   NO
               8   DK
               9 M NA

RACDIF4   DIFFERENCES DUE TO LACK OF WILL
           On average Blacks have worse jobs, income, and housing than white people. Do
           you think these differences are mainly because most Blacks just don't have
           the motivation or will power to pull themselves up out of poverty?
           Missing Values: 0, 9
           Value   Label
               0 M NAP
               1   YES
               2   NO
               8   DK
               9 M NA

RACE   RACE OF RESPONDENT
           What race do you consider yourself?
           Value   Label
               1   WHITE
               2   BLACK
               3   OTHER

RACPRES   WOULD VOTE FOR BLACK PRESIDENT
           If your party nominated a Black for president, would you vote for him if he
           were qualified for the job?
           Missing Values: 0, 9
           Value   Label
               0 M NAP
               1   YES
               2   NO
               8   DK
               9 M NA

RACWORK   RACIAL MAKEUP OF WORKPLACE
           Are the people who work where you work all white, mostly white, about half
           and half, mostly black, or all black?
           Missing Values: 0, 9
           Value   Label
               0 M NAP
               1   ALL WHITE
               2   MOSTLY WHITE
               3   HALF WHITE-BLACK
               4   MOSTLY BLACK
               5   ALL BLACK
               6   WORKS ALONE
               8   DON'T WORK
               9 M NA

RELIG   RS RELIGIOUS PREFERENCE
            What is your religious preference? Is it Protestant, Catholic, Jewish, some
            other religion, or no religion.
            Missing Values: 9
            Value   Label
               1   PROTESTANT
               2   CATHOLIC
               3   JEWISH
               4   NONE
               5   OTHER
               8   DK
               9 M   NA

RICHWORK   IF RICH, CONTINUE OR STOP WORKING
            If you were to get enough money to live as comfortably as you would like for
            the rest of your life, would you continue to work or would you stop working?
            Missing Values: 0, 9
            Value   Label
               0 M   NAP
               1   CONTINUE WORKING
               2   STOP WORKING
               8   DK
               9 M   NA

RIFLE   RIFLE IN HOME
            Do you happen to own a rifle?
            Missing Values: 0, 9
            Value   Label
               0 M   NAP
               1   YES
               2   NO
               3   REFUSED
               8   DK
               9 M   NA

SEI   RESPONDENT SOCIOECONOMIC INDEX
            Missing Values: .0, 99.8, 99.9
            Value   Label
              .0 M   NAP
            99.8 M   DK
            99.9 M   NA

SEX   RESPONDENTS SEX
            Value   Label
               1   MALE
               2   FEMALE

SEXEDUC   SEX EDUCATION IN PUBLIC SCHOOLS
            Would you be for or against sex education in the public schools?
            Missing Values: 0, 9
            Value   Label
               0 M   NAP
               1   FAVOR
               2   OPPOSE
               3   DEPENDS
               8   DK
               9 M   NA

SEXFREQ   FREQUENCY OF SEX DURING LAST YEAR
           About how ofen did you have sex during the last 12 months?
           Missing Values: *, 9
           Value   Label
           -1 M   NAP
            0   NOT AT ALL
            1   ONCE OR TWICE
            2   ONCE A MONTH
            3   2-3 TIMES A MONTH
            4   WEEKLY
            5   2-3 PER WEEK
            6   4+ PER WEEK
            8   DK
            9 M   NA

SEXHAR   R EXPERIENCED SEXUAL HARRASSMENT
           Sometimes at work people find themselves the object of sexual advances,
           propositions, or unwanted sexual discussions from co-workers or supervisors.
           The advances sometimes involve physical contact and sometimes just involve
           sexual conversations. Has this ever happened to you?
           Missing Values: 0, 9
           Value   Label
            0 M   NAP
            1   YES
            2   NO
            3   NEVER HAVE WORKED
            8   DK
            9 M   NA

SEXSEX5   SEX OF SEX PARTNERS LAST FIVE YEARS
           Have your sex partners in the last five years been...
           Missing Values: 0, 9
           Value   Label
            0 M   NAP
            1   EXCLUSIVELY MALE
            2   BOTH MALE AND FEMALE
            3   EXCLUSIVELY FEMALE
            8   DK
            9 M   NA

SOCBAR   SPEND EVENING AT BAR
           Would you use this card and tell me which answer comes closest to how often
           you do the following things...go to a bar or tavern?
           Missing Values: *, 9
           Value   Label
           -1 M   NAP
            1   ALMOST DAILY
            2   SEV TIMES A WEEK
            3   SEV TIMES A MNTH
            4   ONCE A MONTH
            5   SEV TIMES A YEAR
            6   ONCE A YEAR
            7   NEVER
            8   DK
            9 M   NA

SPANKING   FAVOR SPANKING TO DISCIPLINE CHILD
           Do you strongly agree, agree, disagree, or strongly disagree that it is
           sometimes necessary to discipline a child with a good, hard spanking?
           Missing Values: 0, 9
           Value   Label
               0 M   NAP
               1   STRONGLY AGREE
               2   AGREE
               3   DISAGREE
               4   STRONGLY DISAGREE
               8   DK
               9 M   NA

SUICIDE1   SUICIDE IF INCURABLE DISEASE
           Do you think a person has the right to end his or her own life if this
           person...has an incurable disease?
           Missing Values: 0, 9
           Value   Label
               0 M   NAP
               1   YES
               2   NO
               8   DK
               9 M   NA

SUICIDE2   SUICIDE IF BANKRUPT
           Do you think a person has the right to end his or her own life if this
           person...has gone bankrupt?
           Missing Values: 0, 9
           Value   Label
               0 M   NAP
               1   YES
               2   NO
               8   DK
               9 M   NA

SUICIDE3   SUICIDE IF DISHONORED FAMILY
           Do you think a person has the right to end his or her own life if this
           person...has dishonored his or her family?
           Missing Values: 0, 9
           Value   Label
               0 M   NAP
               1   YES
               2   NO
               8   DK
               9 M   NA

SUICIDE4   SUICIDE IF TIRED OF LIVING
            Do you think a person has the right to end his or her own life if this
            person...is tired of living and is ready to die?
            Missing Values: 0, 9
            Value   Label
               0 M   NAP
               1   YES
               2   NO
               8   DK
               9 M   NA

TAXMID   TAXES ON MIDDLE INCOME PEOPLE TOO HIGH
            Generally, how would you describe taxis in America today...We mean all taxes
            together, including social security, income tax, sales tax and the rest...for
            those with middle incomes are taxes...
            Missing Values: 0, 9
            Value   Label
               0 M   NAP
               1   MUCH TOO HIGH
               2   TOO HIGH
               3   ABOUT RIGHT
               4   TOO LOW
               5   MUCH TOO LOW
               8   CANT CHOOSE
               9 M   NA

TAXPOOR   TAXES ON LOW INCOME PEOPLE TOO HIGH
            Generally, how would you describe taxis in America today...We mean all taxes
            together, including social security, income tax, sales tax and the rest...for
            those with low incomes are taxes...
            Missing Values: 0, 9
            Value   Label
               0 M   NAP
               1   MUCH TOO HIGH
               2   TOO HIGH
               3   ABOUT RIGHT
               4   TOO LOW
               5   MUCH TOO LOW
               8   CANT CHOOSE
               9 M   NA

TAXRICH   TAXES ON HIGH INCOME PEOPLE TOO HIGH
            Generally, how would you describe taxis in America today...We mean all taxes
            together, including social security, income tax, sales tax and the rest...for
            those with high incomes are taxes...
            Missing Values: 0, 9
            Value   Label
               0 M   NAP
               1   MUCH TOO HIGH
               2   TOO HIGH
               3   ABOUT RIGHT
               4   TOO LOW
               5   MUCH TOO LOW
               8   CANT CHOOSE
               9 M   NA

TVHOURS   HOURS PER DAY WATCHING TV
               On the average day, about how many hours do you personally watch television?
           Missing Values: -1, 99, 98
           Value   Label
               -1 M NAP
               98 M DK
               99 M NA

XMARSEX   SEX WITH PERSON OTHER THAN SPOUSE
               What is your opinion about a married person having sexual relations with
               someone other than the marriage partner — is it always wrong, almost always
               wrong, wrong only sometimes, or not wrong at all?
           Missing Values: 0, 9
           Value   Label
                0 M NAP
                1   ALWAYS WRONG
                2   ALMST ALWAYS WRG
                3   SOMETIMES WRONG
                4   NOT WRONG AT ALL
                5   OTHER
                8   DK
                9 M NA

ZODIAC   RESPONDENTS ASTROLOGICAL SIGN
           Missing Values: 0, 99
           Value   Label
                0 M NAP
                1   ARIES
                2   TAURUS
                3   GEMINI
                4   CANCER
                5   LEO
                6   VIRGO
                7   LIBRA
                8   SCORPIO
                9   SAGITTARIUS
               10   CAPRICORN
               11   AQUARIUS
               12   PISCES
               98   DK
               99 M NA

APPENDIX 3: VARIABLE LABEL ABBREVIATIONS

Abbreviation	Text
Admits	Admissions
Alc&Drug	Alcohol and drug
Ann	Annual
Avg	Average
Brd	Board
DK	Don't Know
Defin	Definitely
Ed	Education
Elem	Elementary
Exp	Expenditures
Gvt	Government
Hisp	Hispanic
Hrly	Hourly
Imp	Important
Institut	Institution
Loc	Local
LT	Less than
Mthly	Monthly
NA	No answer
NAP	Not applicable
Nrly	Nearly
Pop	Population
Pref	Prefers
Prob	Probably
Prog	Program
Rm	Room
R	Respondent
Sec	Secondary
Sev	Several
SqMi	Square Mile
Treat	Treatment
Univ	University

Permissions

Variables in the STATES.SAV data are used by permission from Kathleen O'Leary Morgan and Scott Morgan (1997) *State Rankings 1997*, Morgan Quitno, Lawrence, Kansas.

Variables in the GSS96.SAV data are used by permission from the *Roper Center for Public Opinion Research*, Storrs, Ct. and the National Opinion Research Center at the University of Chicago, Chicago, IL.

Variables HST329 and HTS330 are based on data originally produced in *Physician Characteristics and Distribution in the U.S.*, American Medical Association, copyright 1996-97. As reproduced in *State Rankings 1997* (Morgan Quitno 1997). Used by permission of the AMA.

Variables SCS124, SCS126, SCS127, SCS 128, SCS129, SCS130, and SCS142 are based on data originally produced in National Education Association, *1995-96 Estimates of School Statistics* as reproduced in *State Rankings 1997* (Morgan Quitno 1997). Used by permission of the NEA.

Variables HTS358, HTS359, HTS360, HTS361 are reprinted by permission of the American Cancer Society, Inc. as reproduced in *State Rankings 1997* (Morgan Quitno 1997). Used by permission of the ACS.